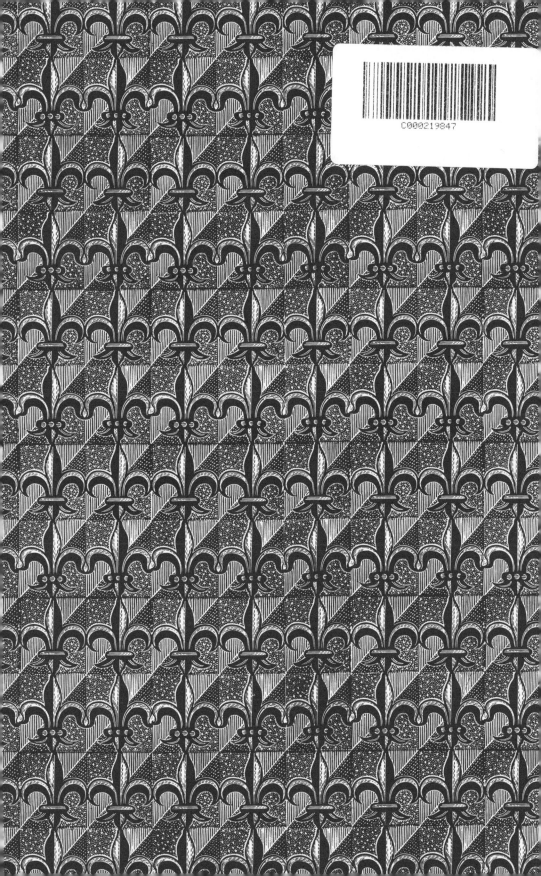

Landlocked

LANDLOCKED

In Pursuit of the Wild

Richard Mabey

SINCLAIR-STEVENSON

The illustrations at the beginning of each of the parts
of this book are:
a detail from Simon Lewty's
Parish Map (Old Milverton), courtesy of Common Ground (page 3);
Frank Newbould's World War II poster *Your Britain.*
Fight for it now (The South Downs), courtesy of the
Imperial War Museum (page 63); Andy Goldsworthy's
Sycamore leaf sculpture, courtesy of the artist (page 129);
and *White water-lily in the Lake District (Little Langdale)*
by Tony Evans (page 191).

First published in Great Britain in 1994
by Sinclair-Stevenson
an imprint of Reed Consumer Books Ltd
Michelin House, 81 Fulham Road, London SW3 6RB
and Auckland, Melbourne, Singapore and Toronto

A CIP catalogue record for this book
is available at the British Library
ISBN 1 85619 432 9

Typeset by Falcon Graphic Art Ltd
Wallington, Surrey
Printed and bound in Great Britain
by Clays Ltd, St Ives plc

Contents

Foreword

Over the past decade I have found that so-called occasional writing has been the most faithful register of the idea that has preoccupied me above all others during this period: the pull of *wildness*, of the spontaneity, inventiveness and sheer serendipity of nature. Wildness is one of the distinctive qualities of the natural world, yet one that the environmental movement has largely (and with not a little embarrassment) passed by. The admission that nature can be a creative, resilient and, above all, independent force is not always a comfortable one for those who see its identity as entirely at the mercy of humans, either as wreckers or saviours. This is especially true in Britain, where so much of the superficial structure of the natural landscape seems to be the product of human activity.

Landlocked is a collection of pieces around this theme, ranging across natural history, travel and art. Much of it, inevitably, is an implicit argument for the independence of nature, but not, I hope, for some all-encompassing, vague greenness. There has been a movement over recent years towards an appreciation of what is called 'the spirituality' of nature, which is contrasted with the materialistic perspective of industry, science and modern farming. It is an understandable sentiment, but I am increasingly unsure what it stands for. Nature, in this generalised and ethereal view, has so lost its roots in the brilliant, complex and diverse world of real

I

living things that it might just as well already be a myth. I hope the pieces here reflect my own delight in the uniqueness and sensuality of living things, and a conviction that transcendence can be found (as Thoreau discovered) *in* the material world as much as beyond it.

I hope they may also demonstrate that occasional, and not always premeditated, writing can be an apt vehicle for such feelings. It is often assumed that essays, reviews, biographical portraits – the bread and butter of most authors' lives – are somehow incidental to serious work on The Books. It has never seemed remotely like this to me. However it originates, jobbing work has to fit in with and reflect the ordinary rhythms of a writer's life, the places visited and people met, the enthusiasms and obsessions that don't vanish just because you have a deadline. As a consequence it can become as much part and parcel of your daily concerns as gardening or friendship; maybe the most *natural* kind of writing.

Part One is concerned with 'Landscape' itself, the real stuff, with the various ways we look at it, and with the prevailing myths about our role in making it.

Part Two, 'Landfalls', is a collection of pieces on places, both at home and abroad. It is about the quality of local distinctiveness that makes each place unique, and how this differs from the abstractions of 'the view'.

The pieces in Part Three, 'Land-Art', are about the links between creativity in natural evolution and in human art. Some are portraits of individual artists (particularly those often described as land or environmental artists), and the majority were commissioned by the journal *Modern Painters*.

Part Four, 'Landmarks – A Sense of Occasion', is a notional year's journal, whose form I hope catches the sense of being 'struck' by the spontaneity (but also the deep seasonal rhythms) of feral happenings. They are edited from a regular column in *BBC Wildlife* magazine.

Richard Mabey
Berkhamsted, 1994

PART ONE

Landscapes

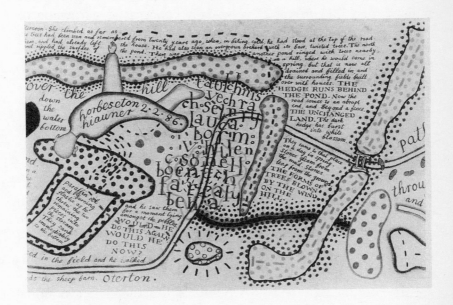

Landscape: The Real Stuff

What is landscape? Is it, as Adam Nicolson has suggested, not a real thing at all but 'an aesthetic category'? Not mountain ranges and water meadows but the emotional patterns we make with these in our minds? Edward Thomas had one kind of answer. When Thomas enlisted in the Artists' Rifles in 1915, Eleanor Farjeon asked what he thought he was fighting for. 'Literally for this,' he replied, picking up a handful of unimpeachably English earth. With hindsight it seems a naive and theatrical gesture. But one knows what he was getting at. The soil – *the* landscape – has always been looked to as a cultural bedrock in times of trouble, a repository of history and a source of inspiration as well as subsistence. It is that strained word 'literally' which sounds so disingenuous, by the side of Thomas's transparently symbolic gesture.

But then landscapes, for all their intricate, living detail, are forever being squeezed down to abstractions and generalities. They are distilled for essences, bottled as heritage and then offered up as 'literal' patches of the real world. The landscapes themselves, not to mention the cultures they support, are made poorer and more vulnerable in the process.

The real stuff of landscape can't be pinned down so easily. Not far from the Hampshire chalk hills prowled over by Thomas is another celebrated landscape – the long stretch of wooded shoreline between Lyme Regis and Axmouth, known universally as the Undercliff. It is a wild and Romantic place of ivy-draped rocks and wind-bent ash trees, and the auras left by generations of visiting writers and artists. Jane Austen must have glimpsed it on her visits to Lyme. Tennyson (who once celebrated a more domestic English landscape as the 'haunt of ancient peace . . . all things in order stored') rambled amongst its dark pools and bushy chasms. Most famously it figured as a powerful, liberating backcloth – almost a supporting character in its own right – in John Fowles' novel *The French Lieutenant's Woman*. It is turbulent, as is the way of the Devon coast, but seemingly timeless, and elsewhere Fowles has written of it: 'It looks almost as the world might have been if man had not evolved, so pure, so unspoilt, so untouched it is scarcely credible.'

In William Dawson's 1840 painting, however, it has an almost pastoral look. Inside the amphitheatre formed by the crumbling chalk cliffs is a wheatfield. Reapers are working through it, and people are picnicking and talking in groups around the edge. A Union Jack is being hoisted above them. It is a rustic scene and unquestionably 'old England'.

Its real history is rather different. The events that formed the Undercliff and lay behind Dawson's *View of the Great Chasm of the Axmouth Landslip* are a long way removed from the mythology of a changeless, immemorial landscape. Two centuries ago this was an unexceptional West Country coastline. It was haunted by religious dissenters and the occasional smuggler, and supported a scatter of cultivated fields on top of the cliffs. Then, one night late in 1839, it literally fell apart.

In one sense this was nothing new, as the cliffs along this coast have always been unstable. But the landslip of 1839 was a more cataclysmic affair. A huge chalk floe, six hectares in extent, slid off towards the sea, leaving a chasm into which the next section of cliff collapsed. On top was a sizeable wheatfield, already carrying its crop. It fell more or less intact, the right way up, and on 25 August the following year it was ceremonially reaped. The whole event became a source of wonder and foreboding in the district, and more than 10,000 people came to watch the harvest. The reapers were led by young women, who had been given silver brooches in the form of sickles as souvenirs.

More landslips followed and within a few decades the present landscape of the Undercliff began to evolve – a secret wild garden, benignly Gothic on the surface, but underneath an impenetrable and precarious wilderness. Every year the local rescue services are called out for someone who is lost, or has fallen down one of the covered crevices.

The history of the Undercliff is a dramatic one, but is really just an extreme example of the way that change and tradition, natural forces and human labour intertwine in real landscapes. Any country parish will understand that harvest ceremony of 1840 and the ambivalence that seemed to hang over it – the shock giving way to curiosity, the insistence on things going on as usual despite the chaos. These are the traditional rules of human survival in the landscape. Get the upper hand again, if only for a season. Make the best of things. Celebrate the inevitable. Life goes on. Landscapes have always been looked on to bridge the gap between two opposed sets of human needs: for a haven of continuity on one hand, and for the vitality of nature on the other; for a familiar environment, fashioned by human hands, and then again for something that transcends the man-made and the artificial.

Myths have abounded in this gap, feeding on its unresolved tensions, and nurtured by ideology and taste. One of the most powerful has been the idea of a national landscape, *the* landscape – some spirit or essence underlying and unifying actual landscapes, which symbolises the British (or more usually English) character. It is of course a rural landscape, despite our having been principally an industrial and urban nation since the late nineteenth century. It was not only Edward Thomas who saw this essential England as being what the First World War was fought for. Rupert Brooke recoiled at the prospect of 'English soil' being desecrated, not long before he became a misplaced piece of it himself, interred, as he had prophesied, in the corner of a foreign field. The wheelwright's son and social historian George Sturt thought the 'Prussian armies' were 'outraging England in her ... pleasant cornfields and country lanes'. In letters from the trenches and recruiting propaganda in the home villages, the notion of what was being defended was repeatedly reduced to a small cluster of familiar rural images: the Downs; stooks glowing in a field at sunset; the call of rooks flying home to a vicarage copse; wild roses in the hedges ... a country wholly identified with its countryside.

Similar feelings surfaced in the Second World War, and were tapped by the Ministry of Information in their campaigns to boost morale. 'Your Britain. Fight for it now' runs the caption over a celebrated Frank Newbould watercolour of what is unmistakably the South Downs. The view is from the top of a hill looking down. In the foreground a shepherd is leading his flock over the open hills, back to a village in the valley. A big, double-chimneyed manor house nestles in a billowing crescent of oak trees. In the distance there are more soaring downs, a lighthouse and, just glimpsed between the hills, the English Channel, the last ditch between us and the enemy. The picture captures the character of the English landscape of popular mythology, and implies that this was part of all the people's heritage. But in what sense was this true? What exactly did that phrase 'Your Britain' mean? Not the privilege of ownership, of course. Nor that we had a right of access. Nor, for the majority of British town dwellers whose landscapes were being destroyed nightly in the Blitz, was it any part of their ordinary, direct experience. Its heart of course was in the right place in suggesting that landscape transcends land as property, and does indeed 'belong' to the people, as do the cultural qualities it expresses – fertility, stewardship of the land, peace, space and continuity. But, as on every occasion when this generalised appeal has been made, the intricate fibre of real landscapes and the lives they encompassed was glossed over.

Fifty years on, during which time the character and working life of the Downs had changed dramatically, Newbould's picture was used again, in a campaign by the Council for the Protection of Rural England. The slogan was the same – 'Your Britain. Fight for it now', but this time the enemy, as everyone understood, was closer to home.

What gives a particular landscape its identity? Over the centuries local patterns of farming and vegetation on these famous Downland slopes have been repeatedly transformed. The hills were covered with trees 6,000 years ago and almost devoid of them in the seventeenth century. Settlements built in times of plenty have vanished during plagues and recessions – or if they happened to spoil the view from the Big House. In prehistoric times small arable fields would have been cleared straight from the wildwood, especially near the foot of the hills. In the medieval periods, sheep took over many of the hills, and their grazing produced a classic, flower-rich, short-turfed pasture. During the Agricultural Revolution of the eighteenth and early nineteenth centuries, much of this was ploughed up for turnips and then wheat – only to revert back to grassland, and then scrub and wood, during the long agricultural depression of the Victorian era. This century the Downs have been cleared and ploughed again, for barley, kale and oil-seed rape. The view from the top of the hill has stayed much the same. But each one of those shifts in the balance between wood, grass, arable crop and human settlement meant dramatic changes in the local ecology and social life; and doubtless every one of them was mourned at the time as spelling the end of the old order. Which stage represents the 'true' landscape of the Downs? Who decides?

But if evolving landscapes are often viewed as immemorial, so there are ancestral habitats which are seen as ephemeral human constructs. Next to the South Downs, for example, is the densely wooded region known as the Weald. An abundance of archaeological and ecological evidence has confirmed that there has been a more or less continuous woodland cover here since the end of the last ice age, and that many individual woods are direct and unplanted (albeit greatly modified) descendants of the wildwood. Yet the myth persists here, as throughout the wooded areas of Britain, that woods derive from, and can only be sustained by, the planting of trees by humans.

What links these two seemingly contradictory myths, I believe,

9

is their common denial of any independence to the natural landscape. It is either appropriated for an abstract, generalised idea of 'heritage' or claimed as the product of benign human stewardship.

Landscape is an old idea but a comparatively new word, and part of the confusion it causes is a consequence of not having a comfortably settled meaning. The term came originally from the Dutch *landschap*, meaning a region or province, plain and simple. It entered the English language (as 'landskip' originally) in the seventeenth century as a piece of fashionable artistic jargon, and, despite 300 years of currency in the turbulent world of rural affairs, it has never quite lost that slightly precious air of the salon. Landscape may imply more than the view, but in one kind of usage it is always *out there*, remote and painterly, exterior design on a grand scale. The same could be said of the putative landscape 'designer', who is perhaps seen as a benevolent landowner, perhaps God, or just occasionally nature itself, as an equally remote force. What is barely even conceived of is landscape as a vernacular production, made in a rather haphazard way by *us*, nature and the weather.

Yet there is another, more anciently rooted sense of place which has no satisfactory English word to describe it. This is landscape as the home ground, the native patch which becomes familiar by being experienced from ground level, landscape as something you look out *from*, not at. This is the way we look at the outside world when we are children, and it can turn ordinary waste patches and favourite trees into whole kingdoms. The poet John Clare wrote unaffectedly of what he called 'pleasant places', and though, for him, they were intensely personal and local, they make a list with universal appeal:

> Old stone pits with veined ivy overhung
> Wild crooked brooks o'er which was rudely flung
> A rail and plank that bends beneath the tread
> Old narrow lanes where trees meet overhead

Yet all such intimate, interior landscapes are set in objective environments of rock, vegetation and climate that change enormously from one corner of Britain to another. Many of these

10

physical features are entirely natural, and seem to permeate the character of different regions however much they have been overlaid or modified by human activity: the stark angles of granite country, for instance, and the softer swells of chalk and limestone; stiff red earth in the Welsh border country, sandstorms in the East Anglian Breckland. Over these regional languages, the intimate local details are inscribed like dialects, and only become intelligible (and often visible) close-to.

Hedges, often regarded as the most defining of all our native landscape features, are a case in point. From a distance they have no identity beyond their functional role as boundaries: they are the grid lines that divide up the fabled English 'chequerboard'. Yet they are hugely varied in age and character: the turf and stone banks – 'reaves' – that separate the narrow Bronze Age fields of Dartmoor; the beech hedges round the windswept edges of Exmoor, and the even taller ones rooted like mangroves along the banked lanes of Somerset's Blackdown Hills; the hedgerow hollies planted – or simply tolerated – as ploughing guideposts in East Anglia; the tall, double shelter belts of the Sussex Weald known as 'shaws'; the hedges that are all that is left of whole woods, and which are evocatively known as 'woodland ghosts'.

The intensely local character of these living boundaries is marvellously illustrated by William Cobbett's description of the hedge-scape of west Hertfordshire in 1822: 'the custom is in this part . . . to leave a border round the ploughed part of the fields to bear grass and to make hay from, so that, the grass being now made into hay, every corn field has a close mowed grass walk about ten feet wide all round it, between the corn and the hedge. This is most beautiful! The hedges are now full of shepherd's rose, honeysuckles and all sorts of wild flowers; so that you are upon a grass walk, with this most beautiful of all flower gardens and shrubberies on your one hand, and with the corn on the other . . . Talk of pleasure-grounds indeed! What that man ever invented, under the name of pleasure-grounds, can equal these fields in Hertfordshire?' It is not difficult to see why this landscape was (and still is) so appealing. It had corn and flowers, productivity and decoration. There were more subtle virtues, too: human ingenuity, a tangy sense of place, a frugal use of resources. It was diverse rather than specialised. It made use of the variety thrown up by nature rather than overriding it.

Boundary features like this are conventionally attributed to deliberate plantings during the heyday of Parliamentary Enclosure in the late eighteenth and nineteenth centuries. In fact most of them are vastly older. Less than a fifth of England was enclosed by Parliamentary Award, and the majority of our hedges are the result of piecemeal enclosures going back as far as the Bronze Age. Many were never planted at all. They began life as strips of natural woodland which were left after a field had been cut out of the forest. Others were the result of shrubs naturally colonising the lines of staked, 'dead' hedges that were features of the landscape even before the Normans arrived. In fact most hedges are a kind of community that the strict hierarchies of landscape mythology don't care to admit – a symbiosis, a partnership between humans and nature.

So are heathlands, but here the mythology is of a primeval, naturally formed wilderness, which because it hasn't apparently been 'reclaimed' by human work is 'wasteland'. Even Thomas Hardy, whose landscape history was usually impeccable, took this view. His description of Egdon Heath in the opening chapter of *The Return of the Native* – 'A Face on Which Time Makes But Little Impression' – is one of the most evocative passages of landscape writing in the language, yet it still paints Egdon as literally, as well as emotionally, primordial:

> Civilisation was its enemy; and ever since the beginning of vegetation its soil had worn the same antique brown dress, the natural and invariable garment of the particular formation . . .
>
> To recline on a stump of thorn in the central valley of Egdon, between afternoon and night, as now, where the eye could reach nothing of the world outside the summits and shoulders of heathland which filled the whole circumference of its glance, and to know that everything around and underneath had been from prehistoric times as unaltered as the stars overhead, gave ballast to the mind adrift on change, and harassed by the irrepressible New.

Heathland, characterised by sweeps of heather, fine grasses and small shrubs such as gorse and broom, is created by the clearance of woodland on poor soils. And it can only be maintained as heath if the cutting, burning or grazing, be it natural or deliberate, is continued. Otherwise it will eventually revert to woodland, as is happening at the moment to many of the unmanaged heaths of southern England. But variations in climate, soil and natural vegetation across Britain mean that this simple regime produces immensely different kinds of heathland: the dry commons of Surrey and Hampshire, and rain-drenched moors of upland Britain; the cliff-top stands of wind-pruned, sun-burned heather on the Lizard peninsula that may be entirely natural, and the fenny heaths of west Norfolk, so pocked with small-scale diggings and glacial scourings that it is futile to draw any line between which are natural and which man-made. Heathlands, as one modern writer put it, 'represent nature's response' to various human activities. But they are also vulnerable to human activity. The south Dorset heaths that Hardy immortalised as Egdon have been largely destroyed by enclosure and ploughing.

The myth of Parliamentary Enclosure as a creative process, concerned solely with the hedging of the open fields, has been astonishingly persistent. In fact, as well as the Acts which led to the enclosure of four-and-a-half million acres of open field and pasture, there were another 1,893 Acts relating to the clearing and cultivation of more than two million acres of commonland. In almost all instances enclosure involved path-stopping, road-straightening, drainage, the clearance of wood and heath, and a wholesale reorganisation of the geography and economy of the parish.

In this respect Parliamentary Enclosure (despite its strictly local impact) symbolised the processes of centralisation and modernisation that had been gathering pace in the countryside during the 'Age of Improvement'. This is often called the era of 'planned countryside', as distinct from 'ancient' and more organically moulded landscapes. Ancient countryside evolved out of centuries of do-it-yourself enterprise, often involving the whole community. It is asymmetrical and small-scale, and typified by sinuous boundary banks, old trees, oddly shaped copses and tapering commons and greens, whose arrangement reflects the natural contours and vegetation. Planned countryside, by contrast, was set out – on a drawing board as often as not – without much sensitivity towards the natural features of the land or the people who lived and worked there. It is uniform and geometric, a tidy patchwork of rectangular fields, symmetrical plantations, straight roads and low hawthorn hedges. As a landscape style it looks much the same in Dorset as in Durham, and everywhere lacks that human scale and quirkiness which makes ancient countryside so appealing.

Planned countryside in this sense is still created, most conspicuously by insensitive tree-planting programmes. The *imposition* of trees on a landscape, often regardless of the character of the place and the species of tree, is still widely regarded as a conservation panacea. The flowering cherries which adorn suburban streets across the land are now being set down in increasing numbers in deep countryside. Hybrid Italian poplars and weeping willows are planted along wild river banks, and ornamental American oaks on medieval Chiltern commons. Indigenous trees (that help give local landscapes their distinctive character) are often bulldozed to make way for them, just as they are in commercial plantations.

Even in the Age of Improvement itself, though, there were contrary views. In *A Description of the Scenery of the Lakes*, William Wordsworth takes issue both with the idea of a timeless, changeless landscape, and with the lofty presumptions of the landscape engineers. And his ecologically precise account of the way natural woodland colonises a Lakeland fell demonstrates his belief that natural landscapes expressed social as well as aesthetic ideals:

> From low and sheltered places, vegetation travels upward to
> the more exposed; and the young plants are protected, and
> to a certain degree fashioned, by those that have preceded
> them. The continuous mass of foliage which would thus be
> produced, is broken by rocks, or by glades or open places,

where the browzing of animals has prevented the growth of wood. As vegetation ascends, the winds begin also to bear their part in moulding the forms of trees; but, thus mutually protected, trees, though not of the hardiest kind, are enabled to climb high up the mountains. Gradually however, by the quality of the ground, and by increasing exposure, a stop is put to their ascent; the hardy trees only are left; those also, by little and little, give way – and a wild and irregular boundary is established, graceful in outline, and never contemplated without some feeling, more or less distinct, of the powers of Nature by which it is imposed.

Contrast the liberty that encourages, and the law that limits, this joint work of nature and time, with the disheartening necessities, restrictions and disadvantages, under which the artificial planter must proceed, even he whom long observation and fine feeling have best qualified for the task.

Wordsworth was in no way hostile to humans shaping the landscape. Yet the point he was making about the vitality and particularity of nature, and the contribution that this makes to the continuing evolution of landscapes, has been all but dismissed in recent years. The current 'heritage' view of the rural landscape assumes that historical evolution is *over*, that what we now hold, however precariously, is a landscape fully realised.

And yet there is a perceptible new exuberance in many of our native landscapes. In the south, for instance, there has been a remarkable and unpredictable regeneration in the woodlands devastated by the hurricanes of 1987 and 1990. In northern England, lime-rich tips outside derelict chemical factories are turning spontaneously into facsimile chalk downs, covered with sweeps of wild orchids. (The Cumbrian poet Norman Nicholson celebrated similar makeshift landscapes around the worked-out haematite mines near his home, and even saw mining as an essentially rural industry like the 'harvesting of a root-crop'.)

We are back with John Clare's 'pleasant places' here, those small-scale, distinctive, familiar refuges which perhaps form the best basis for a common language and understanding of landscape. The view from the hill – appropriative, generalised, reducing humans (and most other living things) to inanimate props – has always missed the details of both destruction and growth. The view from the hedge may be more restricted, but it does register the real stuff of landscapes, and the fact that fossilisation is every bit as deathly as obliteration.

1993

Beeched

Can a whole landscape be defined by something as inherently mortal as a single tree species? You might think so if you lived in the Chilterns. For a century and a half the region's woods – and they cover a vast area – have been dominated by beech plantations: pure stands of gracious, even-aged trees whose forerunners were planted for the Windsor chair industry. The guidebook description of these austere groves is 'natural cathedrals' and it is understandable that their current misfortunes are seen by many as a kind of desecration.

They are dying of drought and disease, being munched away by grey squirrels and blown over in gales. Nature seems to be giving a clear message that the beech is no tree for the current English climate. But the region's loyalty to it is unswerving, and an almost superstitious fear has taken root that if the beech goes, so will the entire woodland cover. So, more despairingly each year, the Chiltern beeches are propped up, put into intensive care and replanted when they succumb. The cost in ecological (and economic) terms is enormous. Natural woodland is bulldozed to make way for them; scrub suppressed by brushwood killers; poison laid down for the squirrels.

I grew up amongst the Chiltern beechwoods and share the widespread sadness at their plight. But they have been turned into totems here, mythologised to an extent that their real history and role do not warrant, and, when it comes to a choice, they have been repeatedly favoured at the expense of more ancient, indigenous woodland types. Our attitude towards them is typical of our desire to put living landscapes in aspic (or, in this case, ill-fitting corsets), and is an example of how, when it comes to nature, we forget the extent to which culture influences our views.

A taste for beech has always, I think, been a rather sophisticated, adult enthusiasm. When I was a child growing up in the Chilterns in the 1950s, it was certainly very low on our lists. It was useless for camps, impossible to climb, and really only good for carving your initials on. Our parents also seemed to have rather distant views of it, albeit more favourable than ours. They saw it as the epitome of elegance and classicism, a feminine foil to the ruggedness of the oak (fine timber beeches were always called 'queens', and singing about 'hearts of beech' would have sounded positively cissy). The undercurrent to this was the ambivalent suggestion that the tree wasn't a proper British native, but had been brought here from the Continent by the Romans, regarded in those post-war years as the fount of all civilisation.

The physical evidence of the beech's history tells a rather different story. The earliest remnants are pollen grains found in the Hampshire Basin, and date from about 6,000 BC – about 2,000 years after oaks returned to post-glacial Britain, and 500 years before the Channel opened up. The beech thus passes – just – the key test of nativeness, in being here before Britain became an island. But it was at the northern edge of its climatic range and by the Iron Age seems to have reached a natural limit south of a line between the Wash and Bristol Channel. Inside this zone it grew on all kinds of light, dry soils, though its well-known association with chalk and limestone may have depended on the opening up of these soils by early farmers.

And this is pretty much where the beech remained for the next 2,000 years, give or take a few isolated colonisations and transplantings. In parts of south-east England it may even have become the commonest tree. But it would have grown then in more mixed woods, with sessile oak in some areas, hornbeam in others, and with ash, maple and elm on more calcareous soils. And the beeches themselves would not have borne much resemblance to the tall, straight trees we have come to associate with modern plantations. They were rarely used for building, and were not encouraged to become timber trees. Even in the Chilterns houses were framed in oak. The beech was valued historically as a more basic kind of workhorse. It was an energy source, producing firewood for humans, and mast for grazing cattle. Mixed beechwoods supplied fuel for many Roman ironworks. In the Sussex Weald, beech was the fuel of choice for the glass industry. And in the Chilterns wood cut from pollard oak and beech (and some coppice, too) was shipped up to London by barge, for the city's hearths and ovens.

The form of beech that develops under a regime of pollarding is squat and broad, with the mat of surface roots by which the tree braces itself on shallow soil echoed in a thick bushel of branches above. The trunk is adorned with intricate flutings, scars and knobs where the bark has grown back over the cut surfaces. Three or four centuries ago this was probably the most familiar type of beech in the southern English countryside. It is still visible in some of the ancient wood-pastures in the Chilterns – for instance at Frithsden, Burnham Beeches and Naphill Common – though with stouter and more gnarled branchings now that regular lopping is no longer practised.

During the eighteenth century, a new form of beech entered the currency. The Age of 'Improvement' had arrived, and tree-planting became a passion among the landowning classes. It was a convenient way of indulging in the contemporary taste for 'natural' scenery whilst producing a commercial crop. It also made a powerful statement about the planter's social status and its likely inheritance down the generations – for at least as long as the life of a hardwood tree. But in order for these underlying ambitions to succeed, no one else could be permitted to appropriate or 'disfigure' the trees, and from the eighteenth century on, common rights of pollarding began to be withdrawn in many woods. At the same time, plantations (often including conifers as nurse crops) began to replace mixed and naturally sprung woods. They coaxed into being a form of beech less familiar than the gnarled old pollards – a tall, straight-trunked, high-branching tree, a Palladian column in wood that soon found an apt economic role in the burgeoning furniture industry.

These changing economic and social roles influenced (and were influenced by) aesthetic judgements. The elegant, investment beech was looked on as beautiful precisely because it *was* economically desirable. (As late as the 1820s even Cobbett maintained that he had 'no idea of picturesque beauty separate from the fertility of the soil'.) It was then only a matter of time before plantation beechwoods were believed to be the correct, normal vegetation of chalk-hill country, and in some ways more 'natural' than mutilated pollards – however Gothic and picturesque the latter might appear.

In the Chilterns they are *still* widely believed to be the 'natural' tree cover, despite the longer and historically richer ancestries of ancient, mixed woods and the few remaining stands of 'vulgar' pollards. I am fortunate in having one of the latter as a neighbour, the venerable waste of Frithsden Beeches, which has had such an eventful history as a wooded common. It was already predominantly beech in the mid-fourteenth century, and there is a telling record of the Black Prince looting some of the commoners' pollards, in order to pay for imported oak for a deer-park fence. And there was a famously unsuccessful attempt at enclosure in 1866, when Lord Brownlow's four miles of illegal fencing were torn down by London navvies. (The court case which followed marked a turning point in legislation to protect commonland.)

Even now the Beeches is a hectic place, a catacomb of immense, contorted pollards, fused and frost-cracked branches, aerial ponds, old graffiti, natural gargoyles and glowering faces glimpsed in the trunks. It is as far from being a 'natural cathedral' as you can imagine, and a lesson in how exciting woods can be when they are not kept under too close a rein.

Ironically, the cessation of pollarding in the mid-nineteenth century has led to the trees becoming top heavy, and more and more are blown over every winter. But natural regeneration of beech, birch and holly in the resultant gaps is spectacular (just as it is – with ash, cherry and maple – in the storm-blown plantations elsewhere in the hills). And, despite opposition from hard-line foresters, the National Trust (owner of the land) is experimentally pollarding some young beeches to replace them, in a fascinating marriage of rescue archaeology and woodland conservation.

I hope we can hang on to good numbers of beeches in the Chilterns – especially in historic and ancient woods. But I hope too that we remember how much their present status is a product of social posturing and commercial convenience in the not-so-distant past, and that we make room for more of the anciently indigenous mixed Chiltern woods. The identity of the region lies in the shape of the hills, in its hidden dry valleys and dark ridge-woods, in flint-drifts and hollow lanes, and on a long human tradition of commoning. It doesn't depend on maintaining one favourite tree as a virtual monoculture.

1992

A Walk Around the Block

It is becoming hard these days to justify the pleasures of simply 'going for a walk'. In a world of sponsored hikes and mass marathons, strolling smacks of introspection and an unhealthy lack of competitive drive. Ambling about with no badges of purposefulness (shell-suits and dogs are the favourites) you are looked on as a figure of fun or, worse, of danger. Children cross the road as you approach. Long-distance trekkers elbow you aside, a cissified obstacle not worthy of consideration. Even the physical act of walking is now being streamlined by the health industry. Going for a stroll, one of the most civilised of pleasures precisely because it can be indulged in purely for its own sake, is now expected to *do* something, either for you or the world.

Yet in a roundabout and less transcendental way this has always been one of the aims of casual walking. 'Just off to stretch the legs,' we say, meaning, as everybody understands, the less mentionable intention of stretching (or relaxing) the mind. Kim Taplin, in her book *The English Path*, recalls the old Latin proverb *solvitur ambulando*, which roughly translates as 'sort it out by walking'. She points out the various connotations of *solvitur* – finding out, working out, freeing, unknotting: all good strolling agendas. It is the combination of gentle physical activity and close contact with the natural world which seems to do the trick. Even the basic business of navigating, of confronting traffic, weather, pot-holes in the lane, seems to help. It may not always be calming, but it does bring you down to earth.

For Dr Johnson and George Borrow, both great wanderers in their time, making contact with the world took on a quite literal meaning during their walks. Both were dogged by recurrent bouts of depression, and to keep some kind of link with reality used to touch objects – trees especially – on their way. For William Hazlitt, solitary walking was a great aid to contemplation, particularly amongst familiar surroundings. 'I can saunter for hours,' he wrote, 'bending my eye forward, stopping and turning to look back, thinking to strike off into some less trodden path, yet hesitating to quit the one I am on, afraid to snap the brittle threads of memory.' Henry Thoreau also relished 'sauntering', and pondered the possible origins of the word in the phrase *sans terre*, 'without land or a home, which therefore, in the good sense, will mean, having no particular home but equally at home everywhere'. He found that he nearly always sauntered towards the south-west 'where the earth seems more unexhausted and richer'.

These ritual qualities, the sense of marking out a territory, are an intrinsic part of strolling. We all have favourite times, occasions and directions for taking a walk, and favourite well-trodden paths, too. Even away from home, a quick turn around the town is always more than just a way of working up an appetite. It is a kind of first-footing, a way of confirming your arrival and getting your bearings. It can also be an act of geographical courtesy, like sampling the local beer, and can give you the same quick savour of a place. In after-dinner constitutionals round hotel grounds I have heard nightingales in Suffolk and found glow-worms in Sussex, edging an ornamental drive. Whenever I go to the Yorkshire Dales in late spring, the village hay meadows on that first evening stroll seem to have a burnished newness, a focus, that later, further-flung tramps can never quite recapture.

But dawdling on foreign territory is when you can look most conspicuously odd and out of place. One Easter in Suffolk, I broke a car journey to take an airing along a footpath that wound invitingly towards a copse in the middle of a barley field. It was an ancient track, banked and ditched, and I rather hoped there might be oxlips in flower in the wood. I left the path, climbed a gate, and sure enough there were. But soon there was also an outraged farmer who had trailed me up the track. I don't think it was my minor act of trespass that had upset him, nor my feeble waving of the Ordnance Survey map as an excuse, so much as the sheer casualness of my arrival. 'You've got a car,' he shouted, 'you could have come to the farm and asked.' It was a sharp reminder of the original purpose of fieldpaths that I haven't forgotten.

You are on surer ground on your home patch, and here the routes as well as the strolling habit can become ritualistic. There are maybe half a dozen walks near my home in the Chilterns that I take regularly, like doses of tonic. One, a mile out and back along a canal towpath, is really a walk of convenience, since it starts just a hundred yards from my door. Another, a short but sinuous tour of a famous wood of gnarled pollards called Frithsden Beeches [see page 20], is a guaranteed cure for moodiness. Beechwoods are conventionally thought of as places for quiet meditation. Not this one. At all times and seasons it is a turmoil of gale-strewn trunks and fleeting patterns of light and shade.

But I suspect the reasons I am habituated to two other local walks are more complicated. Although one is a half-hour hilltop stroll just a short distance from my home, and the other a two-hour river valley circuit ten miles away, they have a lot in common. Both are circular routes. Both repeatedly change their perspective, winding in and out of woods and round doglegs, and opening up sudden new views and hidden glades.

I began making the nearer walk when I was a teenager. I was in thrall to birds at the time, and this short lap was a condensed tour of all our best local habitats. For the first few hundred yards it followed a lane, past fields haunted by grey partridges and sometimes a barn owl. Then it struck off left into a thin strip of woodland where the first chiffchaffs usually appeared and where, if you were lucky, you might glimpse redstarts on migration in the spring. Here and there, through gaps in the trees, you could gaze down into the valley of a winterbourne.

24

Later my weekly (daily, sometimes) trudges round this circuit took on a more intense, contemplative character. I would follow not just the basic route, but my own previous footsteps: along the right-hand side of the lane, hugging close to the dense blackthorn hedge, cutting off the corner by the sentinel beech, turning for home along the field edge, *not* on the footpath just a few feet below. At one point I would always stop and gaze in something close to rapture at the vista that rolled away to the south-west: two miles of hills, copses, chalk scrub and green lanes, with the silver thread of the winterbourne knitting them all together.

In my adolescent years that walk became a bench mark, an arena in which I tested out experiences that seemed important to me. It was a path to take girlfriends along (and, nonsensically, to escape from them). I revised for exams along it, chanting the elements of the Periodic Table in time with my steps. Occasionally, when bird-song was over for the year, I would take a portable radio with me, to listen to the carols from King's College on Christmas Eve, and, in one absurdly romantic gesture, to a broadcast of Beethoven's 'Pastoral' Symphony on a high summer evening – a true promenade concert.

It says something about the character of this walk that it can still cast a healing spell over me, thirty years on. But when I fear that it is too domestic to work, or I want something on a grander scale, I opt for the further walk, down in the valley of the Chess. This is about as far as I would travel for just a stroll, yet, in contrast to my home patch, it has a distinctly southern feel. Bluebells bloom earlier and swallows arrive sooner.

My walk passes through a line of riverside water meadows, sudsy with blossom, where I once saw six cuckoos feeding together. Then it crosses the river, climbs a little and returns along the foot of a beech hanger. The beeches are regularly blown down and with each new gap (and new diversion in the footpaths) there are startling new views of the woodlands on the scarp to the north. They are cherry woods, for the most part, cloaked with white blossom in April, and later ringed by it, when the petals fall and settle round their rims.

There is a flamboyant, southerly feel about the people here, too. It is a popular walk, strewn with picnickers and paraders whenever the weather is fine. One regular plods the circuit in climbing boots, carrying a small dog in his arms. Two others I have never glimpsed, but their polished champagne glasses are hidden high in the cruck of a riverside oak.

Can regular walking round a familiar beat influence one's thinking, become a kind of ingrained memory track that can be replayed at will? It can certainly affect the way one writes. Even a short walk can provide a writer with a ready-made narrative structure just as effectively as a Grand Tour. Yet what is intriguing is how often the *styles* of walking find their way directly into the styles of written accounts. One critic, for example, has suggested that W. H. Hudson's rambling prose 'perfectly echoed the long, slow, unhurried tramping of his feet as he roamed through the gentle southern counties each summer'. Hudson, though, was essentially a tourist, and for me his long-distance ramblings about England echo more with condescension than real curiosity.

Far better, and closer to catching the feel of everyday meandering, is Richard Jefferies, especially when he was producing a mass of effervescent journalism for the new urban audience. The essays in collections like *Round About A Great Estate* (1880) are addressed directly to his audience: 'If you should happen to be walking . . .' many of them seem to begin. It is quite infectious. The reader is taken by the hand and *led*.

John Clare, by contrast, seems barely to consider his readers at all. He is caught up in the immediacy of the moment, or perhaps the remembered immediacy of his childhood; and his many poems which are based on favourite local walks conjure up the image of a boy darting with barely controllable excitement from one side of the road to the other:

> When jumping time away on old cross berry way
> And eating awes like sugar plumbs ere they had lost the may
> And skipping like a leveret before the break of day
> On the rolly poly up and down of pleasant Swordy well . . .

There are others. John Cowper Powys's recollection of the 'sunken treasure' of his favourite field-path routes. John Bunyan's gossipy account of the Pilgrim's progress, which mirrors his own wandering about the Bedfordshire fields and up into the Chiltern heights.

The patron poet of strollers, though, is William Cowper. After his first mental breakdown in the 1760s, Cowper went to live with friends in the Buckinghamshire parish of Olney. Like many before him he tried to keep his melancholy under control by busying himself in active, domestic routines – gardening, walking, looking after his pet hares – and in something close to communion with the physical details of his small universe. 'The very stones in the garden-walls are my intimate acquaintances,' he wrote in a letter of 1783.

All this is reflected in his Olney poems, which pay unfashionably vivid attention to the minute, living detail of the natural world. But it is the structure of his poetry, especially in his masterwork, 'The Task', that breaks most graphically with the contemporary taste for carefully constructed landscape descriptions, and which owes most to his habit of walking. Much of 'The Task' is not ordered to any particular design but offers scenes, observation, reflections exactly as they might be encountered on a stroll. Scale and perspective are repeatedly changing, so that one moment a wild flower is in focus, the next a whole cycle of work in a distant field. One passage in 'The Task', where Cowper is playing games with his own shadow, is a perfect evocation of the state of mind of the habitual saunterer. It captures not only the idiosyncratic viewpoint of the stroller, but, with the lightest of wry humour, hints at one danger that may lurk on the path: the possibility that the rhythmic step and familiar route may become so hypnotic that far from escaping yourself, you become utterly absorbed in it:

> Mine [shadow], spindling into longitude immense,
> In spite of gravity and sage remark
> That I myself am but a fleeting shade,
> Provokes me to a smile. With eye askance
> I view the muscular proportion'd limb

Transform'd to a lean shank. The shapeless pair,
As they design'd to mock me, at my side
Take step for step; and, as I near approach
The cottage, walk along the plaster'd wall,
Prepost'rous sight! the legs without the man.

1988

Beating the Bounds

On Rogation Sunday this year [1992] more parishes will be turning out for the ancient ceremony of Beating the Bounds than at any time since the Enclosure Acts privatised great tracts of the countryside in the nineteenth century.

In the commuter village of Chorleywood Common, Hertfordshire, the inhabitants will perambulate the borders of the 190-acre local common and impress on the younger participants the extent of their shared rights by bumping them at key points along the way. In Charlbury, Oxfordshire, there will be no formal ceremony, but the whole eleven-mile parish boundary will be tramped. In Upton, Nottinghamshire, the procession will skirt four parishes and follow the route of old field-paths to ensure they are kept open. Gainsborough, Lincolnshire, will hold a treasure hunt and distribute 'Rammalation (i.e. Perambulation) biscuits'. On Ascension Day (the Thursday after Rogation Sunday) the parish of St Michael in the Northgate, Oxford, will re-enact its spectacular boundary procession, passing en route through Marks & Spencer, and ending with choirboys scrambling for hot coins thrown from the windows in Lincoln College. And somewhere, doubtless, an enterprising theme park will put on a display of besmocked yokels being dunked in streams and thwacked with willow wands.

It would have been remarkable if Beating the Bounds hadn't been dusted off and added to the swelling almanac of 'heritage' events. But I don't think the revival is attributable simply to nostalgia or a taste for glib spectacle. The ritual of Perambulation has always been most stoutly upheld at times when land rights or community identity were felt to be under threat: during the Civil War, for example, or in the early stages of the Parliamentary Enclosure era. It also tended to be enacted locally when there were boundary changes, or when a new Lord of the Manor or clergyman arrived, as a deterrent to the over-ambitious. The latest revival is squarely in this tradition. It is a response to the continued loss of common land and access rights in the countryside; to the government's failure to introduce its promised legislation to protect these; and to the attrition of the more nebulous quality of local distinctiveness. The Open Spaces Society is basing a campaign around this year's processions, and is stressing the contribution they can make to 'fixing' common and other open land in parish consciousness.

Beating the Bounds has its origins in pre-Christian fertility rites held in the fields, like the Twelfth Night fires which used to be lit in orchards and newly-sown wheatfields in the West Midlands. Giving magical encouragement to growing crops went hand in hand with the reaffirmation of shared rights over particular areas of crop or pastureland, and of the boundaries of the community itself. By the fifth century, Perambulation ceremonies had – along with many other vernacular festivals and rites – begun to be Christianised, and had taken their place in the calendar amongst that great constellation of rural revels that coincide with the sacred May-tide festivals of Ascension and Whitsun. Whitsun Ales, some of the Derbyshire Well-dressing ceremonies, Planting the Penny Hedge at Whitby, Cheese-rolling at Brockworth in the Cotswolds, and many crop-blessing services are all traceable either to pagan fertility customs or to ceremonies to reassert rights over the land. Even Oak Apple Day (29th May), though ostensibly a recent celebration of the Restoration and especially of Charles I's refuge in the oak at Boscobel, has absorbed older May-tide celebrations of wood-gathering rights, as at Grovely in Wiltshire.

It is a comment on how deferential we have become over

30

land-rights that Beating the Bounds (where younger parishioners are often traditionally larruped themselves) is often assumed to be a picturesque lesson about the sanctity of real estate and the virtues of 'knowing your place'. Historically it was more political than this, and was also intended to warn landowners against abusing the rights of commoners and the labouring poor. The Church supported this populist aim, at least to the extent of defending the status quo, and the Homily for Rogation Week gives a stern rebuke to all those who 'encroach one upon another'. It condemns the obliteration of ancient dole and boundary markers on commonland, the blockage of field-paths, and the ploughing of common headlands and walks in the open-field system. 'These strange encroachments', the homily continues, 'should be looked upon, these should be considered, in these days of our perambulations; and afterwards the parties admonished and charitably informed.'

The fully-fledged Rogationtide perambulation was an extraordinary amalgam of civic lecture, Christian sacrament and village junketing. It was led usually by the parson and some of the local tradespeople and churchwardens, and followed by a group of rowdy young novitiates. At various points on the route the latter were bumped against trees or on the ground, and ducked in streams if the boundary crossed water. Crosses were made, fragments of gospel read, cakes eaten and a good deal of beer drunk. Where encroachment was discovered or access blocked, fences were torn down and wooden stakes driven in along the correct (that is, immemorial) boundary lines. The whole affair often took two or three days.

What the Perambulation communicated and reinforced was a kind of mental map of the parish, and of the social relations that existed inside it. In the case of Gilbert White's Hampshire village of Selborne, a written account of the perambulation survives which perfectly catches this complex mixture of aboriginal song-line and Christian benediction. The route was normally passed down through the collective memory of the village, but after the 1703 walk it was inscribed in the Parish Register by

Gilbert's grandfather. This is part of the route prescribed for the afternoon of the first day:

> Leave forked Pond a little on the left hand, thence over the next Hill into the Bottom, keeping near to the Edge of Grigg's Green, and over the moor that lyes on the left hand under Weaver's Down, from thence by a Slade up the Hill towards the east side of the Hill, and then passing over and leaving the top of the Hill a little to your right hand, keep down the side of the Hill to a green way (where you see Foley Ponds on the left) and keeping all along that way on the east side of Iron Barrow or Iron Hill, down to dead man's Thorn, where is also a large stone, near to a road, and here a Gospel is to be read, a Psalm to be sung and a Cross made X.

Another social contribution expected of the Perambulation, also pertinent today, is the opportunity it gave for villagers to talk with one another, and for newcomers to be introduced to their neighbours. George Herbert, poet, rector of Bemerton in Salisbury and legendary open-air preacher, wrote an account of a model country parson's life entitled *A Priest to the Temple* (published posthumously in 1652), in which he lists the benefits of the ceremony, including: 'a blessing of God for the fruits of the field; Justice in the preservation of bounds; Charitie in living walking and neighbourly accompanying one another, with reconciling of differences at the time, if they be any'. These days, when so much mass-walking is either competitive or circumscribed by sponsorship, a division of the entertainment business, 'walking and neighbourly accompanying' can be a genuine contribution to parish cohesiveness.

This was certainly the hope behind the reintroduction of the ceremony in Newton Regis a couple of years ago. Newton is a picturesque Warwickshire village wrestling with the kind of problems affecting many rural settlements at present: farms and shops selling up, employment opportunities declining, the older cottagers being bought out by commuters and other 'outsiders', and a new motorway link with the West Midlands decanting tourists and drinkers into the village at weekends.

In the late 1980s some of the older inhabitants felt that reintroducing Beating the Bounds might help sharpen the village's blurring sense of itself. About fifty people (maybe one tenth of the population) turned out for the first foray and set themselves the modest task of walking about four miles of the parish boundary. It was a garrulous company from all classes and age groups (including ex-parishioners and occasional visitors like myself), many neither familiar with nor dressed for outdoor walking, and the perambulation became more of a Sunday afternoon stroll than a procession. We were led by a retired local woodman with immense knowledge of parish history, but even his continuous narrative could barely navigate us through a landscape that had changed beyond all recognition since the bounds were first established. Ancient boundary hedges had been grubbed up and footpaths obliterated by cereal crops on which the sickly smell of pesticide still hung. Our guide waved his hand bravely at remnants of the old landscape every time we reached another unnavigable drainage ditch or new barbed-wire fence. From time to time we stopped for Rogation hymns and prayers, and at the close of the afternoon the rector stretched his arms wide and gave a Bunyanesque blessing on the entire company of living things that lay within their compass.

But to tell the truth, the assembly weren't that interested in either the bounds or the landscape. What occupied them most was 'neighbourly accompanying' – chatting about holidays and gardens and how the children were doing at school. Telling stories, too: 'We had a day out in London. On a coach. Only it broke down and we had to get the bus. Well, everybody was asking everybody else how they felt and would they be worried back at home, when the conductor comes round. "Good Lord," he says, "what's the matter? Nobody's talked on this route since the war."'

John Berger has suggested in *Pig Earth* that this continuous story-telling – a community's construction of 'a living portrait of itself' – is the distinguishing characteristic of rural village life. Increasingly, in these days of unsettling change in the countryside, the stories centre around the conflict between local knowledge and camaraderie – 'the way we do things here' – and the ignorance and insensitivity of the outside world. They take in, as they did on the Newton walk, the end of the independence and isolation

33

of rural villages, the grim prospect of them becoming nothing more than museum pieces, and what it is that gives a place its distinctive quality. These are big and important issues, and these days 'knowing your place' in the literal sense needs both local, 'inside' (but sometimes vulnerably conservative) knowledge, and the more abstract, expansive but concerned insight of outsiders, what Sue Clifford has called 'tumbleweed expertise'.

Such issues, of course, have always been at the heart of the Beating the Bounds. So as Perambulation revivalists physically contest the most pernicious threats to access to the countryside since the nineteenth-century Game Laws, it may be a comfort to remember that 'walking and neighbourly accompanying' can play its part, too.

1992

The Parish Map

Redlynch is a modest village in south-east Wiltshire, just outside the boundaries of the New Forest. It has no historic buildings or distinguished one-time inhabitants of the kind that guide books fawn over. The reed-marsh after which it was named in Saxon times has long since vanished. On road-maps it is not much more than a kink in the by-roads between Southampton and Salisbury, and I could easily have missed it in the thick fog if I had not been given weatherproof directions of a kind that don't figure on ordinary maps: 'straight on over a rattling cattle grid, right at the Saab garage, look out for the first thatched cottage . . .'

I arrived without a hitch, thanks to Redlynch's flair with intimate geographical details. It is one of hundreds of communities [the figure had passed 1,000 by the end of 1993] across Britain currently at work producing maps of their own parishes, recording details that local people care about. The scheme was started in 1986 by the arts and conservation group Common Ground, and Redlynch opted early on to make their contribution a 'soft' three-dimensional map in cloth. Working in small groups in an attic, volunteers have already half-finished a six-foot-square patchwork of their local landscape which would astonish anyone who assumed that an inconspicuous village must also be a dull one.

Their map is an extraordinary prospect of quilted hills and

muslin valleys, to which a growing number of villagers are stitching affectionately regarded landmarks: favourite views and the routes of evening strolls; a cricket match; poppies blazing on a headland; an ancient path across the high chalk. In the pale winter light the map looked like a lichen-crusted rock, something grown, not made. Beyond the window the real Redlynch seemed insubstantial by comparison, a dim presence obscured by the mist. It was the kind of weather to put map-makers on the spot, and force them to confront two basic questions about maps: what are they for, and are they 'true'?

Nowadays we tend to regard maps in a strictly utilitarian light. They are for getting to places and briefing estate agents. They are expected to be objective and comprehensible, and to shun irrelevant and personal detail. Even the Ordnance Survey – which as a work of minutely detailed geography has no rival in the world – renders all Britain's astonishing surfaces down to a handful of pastel colours. There is no room on this kind of map for those small, idiosyncratic features that give places their individuality: the colours of local stone, a factory window that shines in the setting sun, the best blackberries, climbing trees, a view from a bridge, childhood dens, a maple hedge in autumn.

It is this gap between what is valued at a local level and what is officially portrayed that gave Common Ground the idea for its parish map project. Its principal aim as an organisation has always been to stress the importance of familiar and shared experiences of nature and place, and parish maps looked like an avenue for exploring these experiences at both an individual and a community level.

The project's guidelines are simple and straightforward. The object is to encourage people to look more closely at their own locality and what it contains, and in the process to discover what it is that defines their 'home patch'. The results are to form the basis for a map, of any type or size and in any medium. It might include local architecture, wildlife, remembered events, or just favourite spots, pure and simple. The only important conditions are that the finished work should be displayed somewhere in the parish, and that it ought to try to convey *feelings* about the place as well as physically depicting it.

The project is organised in two sections: parish maps by individual artists, and those by communities working as a team. The eighteen individual artists were selected by a panel of distinguished art experts together with representatives of Common Ground, and are working in a cross-section of environments, both urban and rural, across the country.

Conrad Atkinson has mapped Cleator Moor in Cumbria, just a few miles inland from Sellafield. His montages set photographs of old street names against starkly jotted plans, and past craftsmanship against an ominous nuclear future. Pat Johns from Topsham in Devon has woven a tapestry in the cool, submarine tones of the Exe estuary – herons, seaweed and a Green Man held in a latticework of marshland dykes and creeks. In Blaenau Ffestiniog, the sculptor David Nash has said of his work: 'This map is made with the earth and stone materials of the watershed from Blaenau to the sea, an extended personal parish from my home body to the immediate locality.' Tony Foster of Luxulyan in Cornwall has used the physical stuff of his parish in a more literal way. Attached to his painting of an overgrown quarry are samples of china clay, granite, lichen and a pressed primrose.

Several of the artists' maps are based on London, including a vast, impressionistic and witty homage by Balraj Khanna to his neighbourhood cricket ground, Lord's, entitled 'The Real Centre of the Universe'. But none is more uncompromising than Hannah Collins' study of London Fields. Hannah lives and works in one of the worst areas of inner-city dereliction, a parish still wearing the scars of the Blitz, and now gutted again by poverty and unemployment. She plays with quiet reveries of the small ambit of her working environment – a typewriter, a book on a bed – and with unsettling images of bomb-damaged Hackney. Her parish map is in fact a map of her own room, superimposed on a turn-of-the-century photograph of the vanished shops in London Fields' Mare Street.

A fascination with how the past affects or lingers on in the present landscape is common to many of the artists. So is a compulsion to make some kind of physical contact with their native spot. Perhaps there is something akin to sympathetic magic here, a hope that the *genius loci* may be preserved in a stolen stone or scratched photograph.

The significance of things, rather than their precise position or scale, was the principle which guided most early map-makers, up until the time trade and technology demanded more literal ground-plans. The first aboriginal maps were made of sticks and shells tied together. In the Caroline Islands in the western Pacific, the inhabitants had symbolic charts of their local reefs and islands tattooed on their bodies. In Britain, some cryptic prehistoric rock markings may well represent landscapes. In the Italian Alps they unquestionably do. Many rock carvings in the Valcamonica, mostly between 3,000 and 4,000 years old, are instantly recognisable as maps of local communities, with fields, animals, people at work and in their houses, the last with outside ladders up to the second floor beautifully drawn in. They are the direct ancestors of modern parish maps, social – and maybe religious – celebrations of the home ground. What they declare, proudly and clearly, is: this is the place in which we live.

As yet, there are no modern parish maps scratched on rock. But in Calverton, in Nottinghamshire, villagers are working on a free-standing structure made of local brick and glass, which will carry four mural panels of local life and landscape. Buckland Newton, in Dorset, has produced eight maps painted onto the inside gables of the village hall. There are maps of rights of way, field names, personal places, and even a 'graffiti map' on which anyone can make a mark or comment. As hoped, the project has increased awareness of and pride in the parish. The villagers have beaten the bounds of Buckland for the first time since 1758. They have also exchanged visits with another village in the scheme, Lockwood in Cleveland. This is a new parish, only five years old, and the council, in common with local authorities in a dozen other areas from the Breckland in East Anglia to Uplyme in Devon, sees the parish map project as an invaluable way of forging stronger community links.

38

There has been local-authority support in Redlynch, too, but the map has chiefly grown in an unplanned, rather organic way. The coordinator, Jane Whittle, was determined from the outset that the project would be a truly communal one. Questionnaires and invitations to help were distributed to every one of Redlynch's 900 houses by the milkman. Even the form of the map, embroidery, was chosen because it seemed the natural way for numbers of people to work together using ordinary domestic skills. But perhaps the most remarkable feature of the Redlynch map is that it is being made rigorously to scale. This is a democratic map, on which no single parishioner can hog the stage. The imagination and affection come through in a more subtle way, in the choice of materials to portray the different features. The silver lace streams, the ragged, thick-pile bluebell woods, the gorse and bracken patches picked out with French knots (so like miniature fern-heads themselves), the violent yellow rape field, are tiny components by themselves but speak volumes about the care and feeling with which they have been worked in.

As in Buckland Newton, perhaps the most important effect of the project has been the spin-offs: the enthusiasm of the local children; the vastly increased awareness of (and respect for) their own locality amongst the villagers. As one of them put it: 'Now when I drive about I look for colours and think about the ups and downs and how they join together' – an apt reminder that much of the British landscape is itself an immense historic map, and that many of its features – from Celtic standing stones and medieval hedgebanks to holly trees still used as ploughing guidemarks – are signs of our ancestral need to find our own place in it.

1987

Kew's Hurricane

When the hurricane hit Kew Gardens on 16 October [1987], it was almost as if a bomb had at last hit St Paul's. Our national gardening shrine, a monument to two centuries of natural science and survivor of the Blitz, had been ransacked. The staff were in a state of shock, and their initial estimates were that a third of all the trees in the oldest and most famous arboretum in the world had been destroyed. The gardens were closed to the public indefinitely and the deputy curator declared it 'the worst day in the entire history of Kew'.

In fact the gates were closed for just twelve days. Gardeners are, of necessity, a hardy and resilient breed, and once the staff had cleared a pathway round the gardens and got a measure of the scale of the damage and of the rescue operation required, morale began to rise perceptibly. In the last few days before the public was readmitted, rather calmer autumn skies looked down on a prospect that was now less like a Doom than one of those teeming harvest scenes by Bruegel.

The staff were out in force, sawing, clipping, sweeping, measuring. The resident foresters were still disentangling the tree of heaven which had crashed ceremoniously onto the roof of William IV's Temple, built the year the tree was planted, 1837. Botanists were agog at the sight of whole and hitherto uncharted root systems suddenly levered up into the light.

Throughout the gardens the mood was one of cutting losses and making plans. It was a cheering exhibition of ancient, Georgic wisdom, and contrasted pointedly with what was happening beyond the walls: in Kew village they were talking of holding a memorial service 'for the fallen'; and in south-east England at large the havoc created by the storm had spawned nothing more constructive than laments for a landscape supposedly 'damaged beyond repair', and a rash of hasty, cosmetic planting schemes.

This is not to say anyone is making light of the destruction. Although estimates of the number of trees lost at Kew have been progressively reduced, it still looks as if more than 500 specimens were blown down or seriously damaged. Many of these were of great scientific or historic interest. Oaks planted by Queen Charlotte 200 years ago were toppled, as well as a black walnut put in by the present queen in 1959. Kew's only specimen of *Ulmus villosa*, a vast and promising elm which seems resistant to Dutch elm disease, was lost, as well as less conspicuous rarities like the apple *Malus trilobata*.

Even the more mundane trees – the poplars and limes and mulberries, down in their dozens – doubtless had friends somewhere. I have to own up to feeling a surge of relief when I discovered that the ancient zelkova whose fall had been so publicly lamented was not the one I'd been sitting under a few days before the storm but an older and bigger specimen that had crashed through the Herbarium windows. It was not a creditable feeling, but trees arouse these fierce and irrational loyalties.

Kew has always recognised this. It has a long tradition of fostering the enjoyment of plants as well as their scientific study. Its early years coincided with the heyday of the English landscape movement, and since then it has aspired to be what one eighteenth-century visitor described as 'the Paradise of our world', a centre of excellence for all the horticultural arts. This is why its response to the great culling of 16 October may have lessons for those parts of southern England which have been shell-shocked by the loss of fifteen million trees, and the overnight transformation of their local landscapes.

Trees have been central to Kew's character since its inception. They provide its most elegant specimen plants and diversify prospects that would otherwise seem flat and featureless on this Thames-side location. Even when the site was in private ownership in the late seventeenth century, it was renowned for its trees, especially 'two lentiscus mastic said to be the best in England . . . and four white-striped hollies'.

The complex of gardens that eventually became Kew began to be acquired by the royal family in the 1720s, and during their haphazard growth from pleasure grounds to fully fledged botanic gardens many distinguished landscapers added their personal stylistic flourishes. William Chambers, working for Augusta, Princess of Wales in 1757, created a fantastic potpourri of classical, Gothic and Chinese follies, set amongst belts of trees. Capability Brown added more formal groves in the 1760s, and excavated what is now the Rhododendron Dell. Meanwhile, the more strictly botanical enthusiasms of Augusta and her close friend Lord Bute, and, later, of Queen Charlotte and Joseph Banks, were directed towards building up an incomparable collection of plants from all over the world. By 1780 the royal arboretum covered five acres and contained nearly 800 different species of tree and shrub. The public were admitted on Thursdays, and people came up the river by barge to meander and picnic among the wooded walks.

Kew became an official public garden in 1841, under the directorship of William Hooker, who commissioned W. A. Nesfield to lay out what is basically the present network of rides and tree-lined avenues radiating out from the Palm House. By 1850 the number of specimen trees had risen to 3,500. Kew soon became a favourite weekend resort for Londoners. One Victorian visitor, carried away by the romantic atmosphere, praised 'the odours and fantastic beauties of the tropics, the fairy-like vegetation of a clime more favoured in this respect than our own, and such a bewitching sight of exotic loveliness as may be nowhere obtained'.

It is this legacy of the intermingled tastes and preoccupations of six generations of gardeners that was severely dented by the hurricane. It was not just individual trees that were lost but components of particular historic landscapes. The problems raised by the 'restoration' of the gardens are consequently a matter of aesthetic and historical judgement as much as of gardening skill. Is one seeking true recreation, a historical facsimile? Or a continuation of the spirit of the place? Trees are not like bedding plants. Decades of fashion can pass before they achieve the effects imagined by the planter. Cultivating trees from around the globe is a hard enough task in its own right; doing it so that results satisfy both sentimental tourists and pernickety taxonomists makes the restoration problems formidable.

I was fortunate in being able to walk round the garden with Tony Kirkham, a supervisor in the Arboretum and a man with long experience in both forestry and botanical gardening. Our journey round the wreckage became a kind of forensic trail, of evidence and clues and hints of solutions. It was the suddenness and capriciousness of the storm that had so upset the staff, he complained. Kew loses a few trees every year through old age, disease and minor gale damage. But the October storm had been different. It caused two decades of damage in a couple of hours. It had uprooted ancient hardwoods and left spindly conifers intact. None of the sickly trees scheduled for felling in the winter had been touched. It was hard to see any overall pattern in the damage. Although some families (e.g. catalpas and false acacias) were especially vulnerable because of their brittleness, the worst damage seemed more a consequence of freak local turbulence and soil conditions. With the ground waterlogged in many places after weeks of rain, trees were easily uprooted, and immense hickories and limes lay with half their trunks buried in the earth, as if they had fallen into a bed of putty.

Thankfully, none of the trees lost was in any sense an endangered species, although Kew has a battery of contingency measures for just such an eventuality. It maintains a seed bank and keeps specimens of living material. It also cooperates with other botanic gardens to ensure that there are specimens of rare species conserved over as wide a geographical spread as possible.

The losses at Kew were of a more intimate and personal kind, of

43

difficult specimens which gardeners had nursed through hard winters and wet springs; of slow growers just starting to show their full potential. One of Tony Kirkham's favourites was the Californian headache tree, *Umbellularia californica*, whose leaves contain such concentrations of volatile cyanates that simply bruising them can release enough to give you a headache. Kew's specimen had probably been the largest in Britain. Another favourite was the Osage orange, *Maclura pomifera*. This is a central United States species, hard to grow in this country and harder still to bring into fruit. Male and female trees have to grow close together for the complex fruits, like small vegetable brains, to set. The hurricane, arbitrary as ever, took the female but not the male.

At this point, however, one must ask in what sense any of these trees is 'lost'. Does a tree cease to be a tree just because it is lying flat? A few of Kew's casualties were small enough and had enough of their root system intact to be simply winched back into a vertical position, though this is too risky for large trees in a public garden. But, almost without exception, the uprooted trees were still alive weeks after the storm; and Kew is famed for its skill in propagation from such material, for producing new plants out of old.

Wherever there is a chance of success – and especially with those specimens that have strong historic connections – the fallen trees themselves will be considered as the starting point for the next generation. Occasionally it may be possible to gather ripe seed; more often cuttings or root sections will be taken for growing on, guaranteeing the emotionally – and often scientifically – crucial continuity between old trees and young saplings. The cuttings may be put into cold storage until their future is decided, or budded immediately in mist propagators.

Plant science and the storm interact at many levels. The effect of the salt carried in on the wind, for instance, will eventually be studied. On that late October day after the storm, though, the garden was full of specialists grabbing a rare and temporary opportunity to examine the parts of trees that even botanists cannot normally reach: the roots and the top of the crowns.

We met a Forestry Commission research team examining branches that showed the long-term effects of past wounds and prunings. Elsewhere pharmacognosists were taking samples of the fungi that live in association with the roots of some species of tree, to test for their antibiotic and anti-cancer properties.

Some of the more mature trees – especially those with beautiful, coloured graining, such as black walnut and hickory – are being eagerly sought by timber merchants. Kew plans to use a dozen of the choicest woods to build a commemorative bench for the Joseph Hooker Economic Botany Complex, which is currently under construction. And this is about as far as Kew will go in specifying its plans for renewal.

But in southern England the problems created by the hurricane are seen as more urgent. Already the lanes are crowded with cowboy chain-saw gangs and opportunist nurserymen peddling runtish shrubs. There is opportunism on a high plane, too, with political and civic pressure for fast, publicity-catching replantings. Most notably, the old myth that the classic rural landscape was created two centuries ago by an intense burst of tree-planting by public-spirited landowners has been taken out for new airing, with the clear implication that the time is ripe for a renewed burst of largess, regardless of site, species or community wishes.

It would be wrong to compare the situation in southern England too closely with that at Kew. The Royal Gardens have the benefits of time and an exceptionally skilled and dedicated staff. Yet it also has constraints (most of its trees, for example, won't regenerate naturally as our native species do). We shan't know Kew's detailed plans for restoration for some while, but it's not hard to guess the principles by which they are likely to be guided, and I think they have clear lessons for the rest of us.

To begin with, Kew knows from its own history that the best and most fascinating landscapes aren't planned *de novo* and in exhaustive detail, but result from a kind of aggregation of the needs of different social groups and different generations. It understands, too, that continuity and identity in a landscape aren't conserved by freezing its living components at one particular point in their

45

history, but by keeping genetic chains unbroken, for instance, and maintaining the overall atmosphere and aims. Kew consequently won't try to replant the garden exactly as it was before the storm, or by imagining what the landscape tastes of our grandchildren might be. Just as the most treasured pieces of eighteenth-century landscapes are those where our ancestors – whether peasant or aristocrat – were expressing their needs and outlooks most eloquently, so the best legacy Kew could leave is a landscape which best represents its preoccupations and views in the late twentieth century. This, I guess, would entail fewer individual trees and more groves; more informal, 'wild' gardening, and more plantings grouped by habitat rather than botanical family.

Whatever happens, there should be one more immediate consolation. Next spring, after such a severe and unaccustomed natural pruning, Kew's surviving trees will almost certainly put on a show of blossom better than anything in recent memory.

1987

The Roots of Civilisation

Every Ascension Day, the children from the village school tramp across the fields to our little parish wood for a service among the bluebells. Surrounded by vaulted beech trees, hung with freshly opened leaves, they sing hymns to new life and crops and the mysteries of transubstantiation. The adults on the sidelines, lumps in throats, gaze heavenwards too, and give quiet thanks that the canopy is opening again, undamaged.

It is a touching ceremony, pious and pagan and ecological all at once, whose springtime precursors were held as fertility rites thousands of years before Christ. And every year the question it raises becomes more insistent: if such numinous feelings about trees are so anciently universal and so easily tapped, why are the world's forests – cradles of most life forms and regulators of the atmosphere – in such a state of crisis?

In the hour or so we are in the wood another 10 square kilometres of tropical forest will have been obliterated, burnt along with all its orchids and birds of paradise to make way for quick-profit ranching and mining. By the end of the year another 100,000 square kilometres will have been irreversibly damaged or destroyed, and the pall of greenhouse gases made a little denser.

How can this be? In the clarity of a Chiltern wood in May, it is hard not to feel unchristian rage at those who haven't yet seen the light.

Yet we are in no position to be self-righteous. Our wood is run as a kind of community plot, and a few months later we are back there, knocking over trees ourselves. It is all quite proper, we assure ourselves, just thinning and good management, making space for new growth, producing a crop for local use. But there is no hiding the exhilaration that can grip you when you start working with trees, the satisfaction of a clean fell, the tang and feel of fresh-cut wood. I have seen our helpers – friends of the forest to a soul – saw and strip a tree down with the single-mindedness of jungle ants reducing a dead animal to a skeleton.

Trees are a *challenge*. Their immensity and longevity and sheer stubborn rootedness spark off all manner of agitated responses. To a puritan a wildwood is a barbarous offence, something not yet in a state of grace; to a farmer a waste of tillable land; to a capitalist a resource well past its cashing-in date.

Woods challenge ecologists, too, to crack their codes, and we are apt to defend the opening-out of our Chiltern patch as helping to speed the wood's natural development – enlightening it, so to speak. But underneath I fear that apostles of the New Woodmanship and Malaysian log barons share the same presumptuous belief: that *our* plans for the forest are better than its own.

These contradictory feelings have coexisted since the beginnings of civilisation. In pagan cultures trees could be both symbols of creativity and the refuge of evil spirits, and placatory rituals were necessary when they were cut down. In Europe there was a kind of secular equivalent of these rites of arbitration in the techniques of coppicing and pollarding (developed at least 5,000 years ago, and still relevant today), which took a continuous crop from trees without killing them. What was common to most pre-agricultural societies was a respect for trees, and a thread of common meaning about their significance.

Set against that there has been the overwhelming image of the forest as the enemy – or at least the converse – of civilisation. The deliberate clearance of the European wildwood was one of the most extensive acts of geographical engineering in the history of the world. It was an absolutely necessary prelude

48

to the establishment of Western-style cities and agriculture. In all periods and places since it has been not so much the sensible use and harvesting of forests that has destroyed them as the desire to turn them into other kinds of land.

In the developed world, perhaps in an act of contrition, trees have become synonymous with Green thinking, and planting them is seen as a kind of environmental panacea. Yet that ancient ambivalence is still thriving, to judge by the symbols they provide: olive branches and hearts of oak; the tree of knowledge and Newton's apple; family trees, Christmas trees, the crown of thorns . . . And whenever they cease to behave in the ways we expect we have the vocabulary of human domination to fall back on: 'dereliction', 'overmaturity', 'scrub' – as if trees, the most successful and durable of plants, were incapable of living correctly without supervision.

There may be less of a gap than we like to imagine between our own mixed feelings about trees and the pillaging of the rain forests. It was certainly an exported version of the European creed of 'improvement' which provided the model and the rhetoric for most large-scale forest clearance.

When the Plymouth Brethren landed in North America they found 'a hideous and desolate wilderness . . . the whole country is full of woods and thickets'; and they set about civilising it with chilling thoroughness. Within two centuries their descendants had obliterated seven-eighths of the continent's natural woodland (and whole species like the passenger pigeon) in massacres whose arrogance and violence rival those in modern Amazonia.

Back in England in 1712, John Morton summed up the prevailing attitude when he proclaimed: 'In a country full of civilised inhabitants timber could not be suffered to grow. It must give way to fields and pastures, which are of more immediate use and concern to life.' The same argument is still being used in Brazil, where successive governments have condoned the conversion of a forest millions of years in the making to short-lived grazing, with the facile slogan 'Land without men for the men without land' – a policy which has impoverished both the men and the land.

In the developed world the philosophical conflict between the need for timber and the mistrust of forests was resolved by making trees submit to the disciplines of cultivation, putting them, in many senses, in their place. Some conservation organisations now believe that the best chance of saving what remains of the tropical forests is to repeat this formula, albeit for superficially different reasons. The realistic alternative to rampant plundering, they argue, is not the establishment of pristine forest reserves, which would take no account of the economic plight of the human inhabitants of the forest, but controlled exploitation.

Yet the history of 'controlled' exploitation in Europe and North America – which has been predominantly a centralised and narrowly commercial business with precious little concern about its social and ecological side-effects – hardly inspires confidence in this as a solution for the tropics. It may not be the best vehicle either for accommodating our dawning understanding of the central role of trees in the economy of nature.

It is worth spelling this out in some detail. Put aside for the moment all the ingenious uses which humans have for trees and tree substances: rayons and cellophanes (made directly from wood cellulose); wood alcohol and forest bark mulch; brazil nuts and drugs still to be discovered; windbreaks and flood control; a huge range of chemicals (even more if you were to include those we take from the fossils of an earlier generation of trees). Put aside, too, the vast assemblages of animals, insects and plants (maybe thirty million species) that don't just inhabit the forest but *comprise* it, and whose breathtakingly intricate relationships it is our species' unique privilege to be able to glimpse.

Think simply of the role that trees themselves play in the natural scheme of things. They are the architectural climax of evolution, scaffolding for the rest of terrestrial life, the enduring idea of rock expressed in plant tissue. Collectively they make up an immense bank of the chemicals necessary for life, and above the thin soils of the rain forests, the sole such bank. Collectively they contain two million-million tonnes of carbon – 400 times the amount released each year by the burning of fossil fuels.

If one had to design from scratch the primary vegetation for the planet, to house and feed the other organisms, to regulate the water and nutrient cycles, it would be hard to improve on trees. Even their present depleted ranks still provide the planet's greatest engine for fixing the sun's energy, which they do by converting carbon dioxide and water into living tissue. In one day a large deciduous tree can pump and transpire thousands of litres of water and take up as much as 20 grams of carbon dioxide. In one year the earth's trees make twelve billion tonnes of new wood in this way.

It is a wonderful process of transmutation which helps control the composition of the atmosphere and its suitability for life. Its reversal – the burning of the tropical forests, which both releases carbon dioxide and depletes the major agency for absorbing it – is one of the factors contributing to the now infamous 'greenhouse effect'.

Trees have played crucial roles in the evolution and support of the variety of natural life. They provide food and shelter. Their spatial complexity rivals that of their chemical structures. They are vast elaborations in three dimensions, not just of ever more intricate branching, but of knots, burrs, bark reticulations, rot-holes, layers of moss and lichen. It is impossible to measure the area of a tree's surfaces exactly. It is what is known as a 'fractal' quantity – one which increases indefinitely the closer you examine it.

Finally, they accommodate the passage of time more comprehensively than other organisms. This is part of the biological function of woodiness, to provide a bulwark against transience and death. And as a tree lives and accrues, sometimes for several thousand years, all its experience – of storms and droughts, human lopping and animal browsing – is incorporated, in-grained, as it were, in its physical structure. No wonder that old trees have so often become landmarks and totems for human communities.

Perhaps this is why generalised campaigns to increase tree cover, regardless of place or the feelings of local people, have rarely been happy or even successful. They touch too many of the ancient contradictions between forests as danger, as wasteland, as ancestral havens. As Sue Clifford has written:

> We have given ourselves a conundrum, without answer. The very notion of creating new forests flies in the face of all we know, and much of what we practise. We know their great age, in the geological sense and domestically. We carved ourselves out of the forest in Britain . . . and in our elsewhere lifetimes. And ever since, we have spent our lives in clearings, on farms, in gardens, in parks, by the wayside, even on buildings, trying to stop trees growing. In parallel we have developed a working relationship with trees which has given us great cultural knowledge, affection and wisdom.

Perhaps our newest knowledge of the nature of that relationship may solve the conundrum at last and restore trees to their proper cultural role, as a commonwealth, as far beyond property as the atmosphere itself. Their most important function, we now understand, is simply to stand there, reminding us of the continuity of life, full of cryptic activity, and *breathing*.

I treasure the memory of a four-year-old in our wood one spring, hugging the trunk of an ash tree and whispering softly into the bark. It seemed then and seems now the best possible way of using another living thing.

1988

Devil's Meat

They are, as often as not, my first glimpse of autumn: a box of early, egg-yolk-yellow chanterelles, wrapped in moss and mailed from Scotland by a fellow fungophile.

This year [1993] they arrived in the middle of the Wimbledon fortnight heatwave, and for a day or two the smells of a summer kitchen were muddled with their fugitive apricot scent and the tangs of the peat and pine needles still clinging to them.

It was the eulogy on chanterelles in Dorothy Hartley's *Food In England* – 'sometimes clustered so close that they look like a torn golden shawl amongst the dead leaves' – that first made me notice the sheer sensuousness of fungi. Since then forays in search of them have become one of the more piquant seasonal pleasures, and about the only saving grace of dank weather.

At least sometimes they are. The behaviour of fungi during this extraordinary, sodden autumn has confirmed what capricious and cryptic creatures they are. I'm used to not finding chanterelles down south, but this year most of the big ground-growing species, from fly agarics to ceps, have been late, scant or maddeningly local.

Even an early October trip to the west of Scotland – usually a forager's nirvana – made me wonder if I had lost my instincts. It seemed a well-nigh perfect spot in perfect weather: a damp and venerable oakwood with the leaves already turning, and a day of pure Gaelic beauty, with Gulf Stream breezes clearing the morning mist from the sea lochs. But of toadstools there was barely a sign – except that the whole wood was draped with lichens, beard lichens and oak-moss festooning the branches, and membranous lungwort swaddling the trunks. These are all part fungi, part green algae, living in symbiotic partnership, so perhaps some of the woodland niches normally occupied by more obvious fungi were already full.

Now, a week later, I am back in the Chilterns, and it is monsoon weather again. I am wandering through a storm-racked beechwood, and it is raining so hard that I can see some of the fallow trees actually breaking up in the rain. The rotting heartwood, as crumbly as earth in patches, is dribbling down the trunks. Tiny wisps of peeling bark, prised off further by the black bootlace rhizomes of honey fungus, are being washed to the ground. Many of the wind-thrown trees – mostly casualties of the 1990 hurricane – are catacombs of fungi. Crimped-edge brackets range along the recumbent trunks, tiers of *Pholiota* and sulphur tuft sprout from the upturned rootplates. I can't put names to most of the vaguely buff bonnets that lurk in rot-holes and range in troops on the dead branches, but others are unmistakable: rashes of the tiny beads, purple and pink, of *Ascocoryne* and coral spot; miniature puffballs, the diaphanous caps of beech tuft (bone-china-white until they droop like Dali watches), gelatinous heaps of *Neobulgaria*, black and white spikes of dead man's fingers and stag's horn; and on still-standing stumps, ledges of dryad's saddle. The undersides of these bracket fungi are pitted with minute pores, like a sponge, and rain down spores continuously for half the year. Sometimes, against a low October sun, you can see them blowing from the undersides like wisps of smoke.

Then, on the ground, I spot a branch stained by *Chlorosplenium*. The wood has the same dull turquoise sheen as corroded copper, and oak logs infected by this species were once used in the manufacture of the elaborate veneer work known as Tonbridge Ware. But the fruit bodies exuding from cracks in the wood are something else – more like a ripple of fused cobalt glass than a plant. Inside the branch, thin mycelial threads – the main body of the fungus – will be probing the wood's capillaries, searching for damp patches and water seepage, secreting enzymes (and sometimes dye substances) that speed the dissolution of the wood and make its nutrients available. Having no chlorophyll, fungi are not able to manufacture their own foodstuff, and have to rely entirely on the detritus from other organisms, leached out by water (which is why they are so exquisitely sensitive to pollution carried in the rain). They are one of the vital agencies of natural recycling, permeating plants, soil and even the digestive systems of animals. And what we call toadstools are merely the occasional fruiting bodies of the fungus proper, the tip of an immense and intricate network of threads. Inside a hectare of wood which produces maybe ten kilograms of toadstools each year, there is more than a tonne of this mycelium. In North America single individuals of honey fungus have been found whose mycelium pervades more than fifteen hectares, and is probably 1,500 years old.

Why is it that there has been such a history of hostility towards these plants in Britain? Although hunting for edible varieties is going through one of its periodic spells of fashionableness, it is still a minority habit, and wild species are still too much the subject of popular suspicion to feature in ordinary markets in the way they do across much of the Continent. Our opinion has barely changed since 1627, when Francis Bacon denounced the whole tribe as 'a venereous meat'. By and large we still kick them to pieces in woods, and view their place in the great scheme of things as being roughly on a par with head-lice. And despite their crucial role as natural scavengers and recyclers, we have still paid almost no official attention to what is happening to them. (Unlike Holland, Germany and the former Czechoslovakia, for instance, where studies have revealed catastrophic local rates of extinction as a consequence of air pollution.)

That is not to say that, taken as a family, they are entirely benign. Some, of course, are poisonous, though these amount to less than one per cent of all the species that grow in Britain. Some are implicated in banes like dry rot, asthma and food poisoning. And people of sensitive or superstitious dispositions are sometimes disturbed by the striking similarities which many species show to human organs – brains, ears, tongues, livers and especially sexual parts. But this is true of fungi everywhere, and doesn't seem to have distanced them in other cultures. Robert Graves once argued that our national hostility was a hangover from the time when hallucinogenic species like liberty caps and fly agaric were the prerogative of a priestly elite and were surrounded by taboos. Yet it's a wariness that doesn't occur in other regions with prehistories similar to our own; and my own view is that its roots lie in our estrangement from woodland, the prime fungal habitat.

Britain was deforested earlier and more comprehensively than any other part of Europe. In the early sixteenth century, when our national tree cover was maybe no more than five per cent (less than it is now), the authors of one of the first popular manuals on plant use, *The Grete Herbal* (1526), divided fungi into just two kinds: 'one maner is deedly and sleeth them that eateth of them and be called tode stoles, and the other doeth not'. It was, to say the least, a highly functional distinction, but not exactly confidence-building. Even now forests are seen as symbolic of danger and lawlessness, and it may be no coincidence that the chief distinction in our culture between good and suspicious toad-stools is made not between those that do or don't peel, or turn six-pences black, but between those that grow in fields and those that grow in woods.

What perplexed all early observers, though, regardless of their cultural background, was the question of where on earth fungi came from. Because their spores are too small to see with the naked eye, toadstools were, for nearly 2,000 years, believed to be the products of some kind of spontaneous generation. In classical times, one belief was that they were produced by the action of thunder. Pliny, writing in AD 77, favoured a kind of natural fermentation of the earth. Pondering the origins of the most prized of continental species, Caesar's mushroom, he didn't seem the least put off by the possibility that they sprang 'from mud and the acrid juices of moist earth, or frequently from those of acorn-bearing trees'. In the sixteenth century, his compatriot

John Baptista Porta reiterated in *Natural Magick* (1558) the belief that 'new kinds of Plants may grow up of their own accord, without any help of seed or such like'. But thirty years later he changed his mind, and insisted that 'from fungi I have succeeded in collecting seed, very small and black, lying hidden in oblong chambers or furrows [gills, that is] extending from the stalk to the circumference'. In 1751, Otto van Münchhausen – a real scientist, but with the imagination of his literary namesake – also found and collected fungus 'seeds', but testified that he had seen them hatch into small insects in water, and concluded that toadstools should not be regarded as plants but as the dwelling places of small animals.

Meanwhile the pioneering micrographer Robert Hooke had realised that moulds and mildews were 'nothing else but several kinds of small and variously figur'd Mushrooms'. But he failed to see spores at all, and believed that toadstools were created from 'putrifying bodies . . . by the concurrent heat of the Air [and] excited to a certain kind of vegetation'. It was not until the early nineteenth century that the real mechanisms of fungal growth were understood. The spores are not so much seeds as minute samples of tissue, which expand laterally to become the mycelium – which, under the right conditions, throws up the fruiting bodies we call toadstools.

Despite the laboured progress of these revelations (they were, after all, flying in the face of centuries of mythology, as well as what seemed to be the clear evidence of the senses), the period between the Enlightenment and the mid-Victorian era saw an enthusiasm for fungi grow amongst the scientifically literate middle class in Britain. In the middle of the eighteenth century the first illustrated guides began to appear, culminating in Thomas Bolton's epic three volumes on the history of the fungi growing around Halifax. In 1758 'Sir' John Hill, who has since been generally regarded as a self-aggrandising charlatan, the court jester of eighteenth-century botany, wrote a meticulously observed and sympathetic monograph on one of the greatest oddities of the fungal world, the *Pietra fungaja*:

An account of a stone . . . which on being watered produces
excellent mushrooms . . . The rock-mushroom is a peculiar kind:
and it is constantly this species and no other which the Italian
stone produces . . . The upper part is a mixed yellow and olive
colour; and the surface is broken in a wild but beautiful manner,
into a resemblance of scales or feathers. The under part is white;
and in the pores lie the seeds. The substance of the mushroom
within is firm and white as snow; and it is of a delicate and
high flavour and perfectly wholesome. A great deal of attention
was used in gathering it to see in what manner it rose from the
rock. The mould was removed, and its insertion made bare: it
rose from the plain surface of the stone by a thick and irregular
base which lengthened into a stalk, and thence proceeded to the
expansion of the head. No roots were produced from this stalk
in that part under the mould. So that it drew no nourishment
from thence . . . The mushroom consists of an expansion of that
fungus substance which covered the stone: nothing more.

(The fungus stone is no fantasy. It is a conglomeration of earth or
tufa held together by the mycelium of a bracket fungus, *Polyporus
tuberaster*, and would be a sensation in the conservatory if it were
more common.)

By this time the fungal scene was no longer so mysterious
and alien, and even curates could trade saucy quips about priapic
growths. In 1766 Rev. Gilbert White of Selborne wrote to his
friend Rev. John Mulso about the 'Stinkhorns, or stinking morel,
fungus phalloides' in one of the local woods, adding with a nudge,
'Linnaeus, for a certain reason, calls it phallus impudicus'. Mulso
replied: 'I thank you for your learned Dissertation on the Canker
or Stinkpot. I knew in general that all Flesh was Grass, but I did
not know that Grass was Flesh before'. And at the turn of the
century, the artist James Sowerby described a bizarre fungus (a
Clavaria) he had found in a London cellar: 'It is remarkable for
being luminous in the dark, when fresh, at the ends of the shoots.
Mr Forster doubted whether this phosphoric appearance may not
be owing to some vinous moisture imbibed, rather than a natural
property of the fungus.'

This note of amused wonder was picked up by the Victorians.
The first book devoted to edible fungi, Charles Badham's *A*

Treatise on the Esculent Funguses of England (1847), is full of wry asides on the beneficence of these wonders of creation, from the use of birch polypore for razor strops to puffball spores for stupefying bees. (Though the best note on puffballs – and a classic vignette of Victorian worthiness – comes from a slightly later text on edible fungi published by the Society for the Promotion of Christian Knowledge: 'We have known specimens to grow amongst cabbages in a kitchen garden, and when such is the case it may be left standing, slices being cut off as is required until the whole is consumed.')

The Victorians must also take credit for inventing fungus forays, those agreeable autumnal saunters where identification skills are shared and baskets filled. In October 1869, for instance, thirty-five members (including nine Reverends) of the Woolhope Naturalists' Field Club set out from Hereford on their annual foray. They ranged about the local landscapes by carriage, stopping off at likely hunting grounds, measuring fairy-rings, and identifying a remarkable variety of wild mushrooms: milk-caps, boleti, chanterelles, witches' butter, hedgehog fungi. More than sixty species are listed in the published account of the foray. The day ended at the Green Dragon in Hereford, with exhibits strewn out on the pub tables, and a late lunch of the day's trophies: shaggy parasol on toast, fried giant puffball, and fairy-ring champignons in white sauce. The puffballs especially were voted a great success, as was the day itself.

But in the twentieth century the fad collapsed, and the Victorians' enthusiasm and curiosity began to seem eccentric to the point of foolhardiness. I remember my own nervousness, as I moved on from fantasy chanterelles to real, mutable, mistakable toadstools. I stuck to the obvious for a long time: ink-caps cooked Geoffrey Grigson style (spread-eagled like a starfish over a fried egg); ceps dried in the airing cupboard; and above all, giant puffballs, whose magnetic appeal doesn't seem to have diminished one whit in the last hundred years. I never found a specimen as gross as the one spotted under an oak tree in Kent during the last war, which for a while was believed to be a new German secret weapon.

Five-pounders, lurking like white rabbits under the hedges, were common, though, and I have a pile of snapshots of my own and other's finds, posed on bars or alongside children and cats, as if they were a species of pet themselves. They were delectable to eat, with the silky texture of toasted marshmallow, but seemed to go on for ever, and I wish we had known that frugal Victorian cut-and-come-again tip.

In fact we had to learn many of the old knacks and wrinkles from scratch. I remember my first, belated hunt for field mushrooms on the north Norfolk marshlands, and my naive surprise that they weren't all standing stoutly up like fairy-story illustrations but were mostly hidden deep in the grass, so that you needed to keep your eyes focused just a few feet in front. I also discovered why folk-lore insists that you pick mushrooms early in the morning. It is nothing to do with them being new-sprung or 'dawn-fresh' but a matter of first come first served. We had strayed that morning onto another group's gathering territory, and for the hour until breakfast our combined movements resembled a slow-motion formation dance. We never spoke, or acknowledged each other's presence, but somehow kept a steady twenty yards between us as we slowly quartered the marsh, sneaking hooded glances at each other between periods of intense scanning for the half-hidden white caps.

It was in 1976, the year of a long summer and a famous drought, that our national fungophobia began, at last, to show signs of cracking. When drenching rain finally arrived in mid-September, it fell on ground which had been baked hard, and created what seemed perfect conditions for fungal fruiting. I was quite convinced I could *smell* them growing: ceps in woods, parasols on road verges, and horse and field mushrooms in quantities that hadn't been seen for a generation. Foraging became such a craze that the BBC began issuing regular information bulletins on the radio. By the end of the month the wild mushroom mountain was so huge in my corner of the Chilterns that they were being hawked from door to door by enterprising children.

Those who have become aficionados since then – a growing

number, to judge from the quantity of neatly cut stalks in British woods and the variety of species found on smart menus – will have found that foraging is a captivating business, a kind of vegetarian stalking. But I think it is sad that passions have been directed so single-mindedly towards edible species. The whole tribe is fascinating and more useful than we acknowledge – as the fortunes of the trees in Windsor Great Park demonstrate. The ancient oaks and beeches here have proved rather more disaster-proof than other sections of the royal fabric, and during the great storm of October 1987 not a single one was blown down, contrasting with the havoc wreaked amongst younger, apparently more healthy trees. This was partly because they had been hollowed out by fungal decay, turning the trunks into lightweight, wind-resistant cylinders. And the rotten, pulped wood helps feed their roots – meaning that, in almost mythological style, they are thriving on their own recycled heartwood.

1993

PART TWO

Landfalls

The Nature of Local Distinctiveness

Our sense of locality, I suspect, is rooted as deeply in territorial feelings as in topography. We become imprinted by places, and become familiar with them just as a cat or fox does. We plod out private routes, touch trees and mark (in our imaginations, at least) our special spots – a bend in a road, a gate to lean on, a face glimpsed in a trunk. Loyalty to these marking posts can be fierce and personal, and given without the slightest regard for what is locally distinctive.

Certainly the first place that I got to know and love when I was growing up as a rather gypsyish boy in the Chilterns didn't have a trace of local identity. It was the remains of a country estate at the back of our road. The big house had been demolished in the 1920s, the landscaped grounds were reverting to wilderness, and we neighbourhood kids (and a good many adults, too) treated it as the local common. We stalked it like aborigines, marking out a cryptic network of landmarks, totems, forbidden zones and hideouts. But its random mix of brick piles, bramble patches and parkland cedar trees could have been anywhere from Surrey to Galloway. What was important – and distinctive – to us were the meanings we had given them.

It was not until my late teens that I recognised, with something of a shock, that places could also have an objective character. I was on a first trip to the Norfolk coast (which proved to have its own tangy sense of place), and on the way passed through that vast and mysterious inland sand-bowl called the Breckland. The sandstorms and great bustards had vanished long before, but not the bizarre wind-breaks that had been created in the eighteenth century from lopped and layered Scots pines. These stunted trees, rising from the sandy fields beyond the sinister US bomber base at Lakenheath, were like no other landscape I had seen. It was a desert, an English badlands.

These pine-belts still give me goose flesh when I am driving east, and it is good to learn that they now have official recognition as a unique and defining element of the Breckland scene. But they are also full of irony and incongruity. For a start, they are a more or less alien tree which hasn't grown naturally in eastern England for 6,000 years. They also played a crucial role in the process of Parliamentary Enclosure in East Anglia, which helped to drive indigenous commoners off the land, and helped obliterate the open heaths and mobile sands that had previously contributed to the Breckland's local distinctiveness.

A further irony is that more than a century later, in the 1920s, Breckland became the site of one of the earliest and largest Forestry Commission plantations. Scots and other pines were again planted out in rows in the sand, but this time in vast, dour blankets that were to become a symbol of the homogenisation of the country-side, and of a process that was making immense tracts of Britain from Inverness to Norfolk indistinguishable.

The contribution of nature to local character is often like this, ambivalent, mutable, as likely to be some new, accommodating growth that fits the rhythms and continuity of the place as an ancient presence or heritage cliché. My home town of Berkhamsted is probably named after the birch trees that grow on the acid plateau above the settlement. They still thrive there, but I find I simply cannot think of my home country as 'the place of the birches'. If the trees do figure in my sense of my own patch, they have become an unconscious backcloth, a kind of second nature yet to be put to the loyalty test.

Natural features were often obvious or important enough to

provide names for places, but the names usually outlive them. There are no lime trees left in Linwood or Lyndhurst in the New Forest. The ravens have long gone from Ravensden on the outskirts of industrial Bedford. And despite the annual neo-Celtic festival in Glastonbury, I doubt that woad is any longer a significant local crop (*glasto* is woad in Old Celt). Even when naming features survive, they can seem as remote and cryptic as Latin family mottos on village war memorials. The weed fat-hen is still common enough amongst the sugar-beet fields of mid-Suffolk. It was called *melde* in Old English, eaten as an important staple vegetable in prehistoric and even medieval East Anglia, and probably gave its name to the village of Milden, near Sudbury. A few present-day inhabitants certainly believe so, and about fifteen years ago put up a cast-iron statue of the weed on the edge of the village. It is one of the most unusual and distinctive parish boundary signs in the country, but I wonder what most of the rest of this still predominantly farming community make of it, having spent the last few centuries trying to wipe out plants like this from the fields?

Features as arcane as this may be too bookish or ghostly to contribute to a real sense of locality. Yet those that are striking and persistent can become communal motifs, sources of pride and maybe even passion, something which can join locals and outsiders in a common sense of place. The wild daffodils that have given the country between Dymock and Ledbury the nickname of the Golden Triangle are a good example. A few centuries ago many parts of Britain could have offered the sight of whole copses and meadows lapped with yellow under the March sunshine. Now, it is only a few oases like this stretch of the border country that have the plant in any quantities. It was already becoming a speciality of this region in the 1930s, when the Great Western Railway used to run 'Daffodil Specials' here, and local farmers and fruit growers threw open their fields to pickers. After the last war, the local colonies were reduced still further by agricultural changes, and local daffodil consciousness declined. But there are signs it is picking up again. There are local daffodil festivals, and a remark-able cooperative effort by landowners, local authorities and local people has created a ten-mile walk through woods, meadows and churchyards that is never out of the sight of the 'dancing host'.

Similarly, limestone in the Yorkshire Dales is recognised by native and tourist alike as one of the defining features of the place. It isn't quite like limestone anywhere else in Britain – in Derbyshire or the Mendips or the Brecon Beacons, say. The difference is not just a matter of natural geological features, of limestone pavements and scree slopes, but of what local people have done with the stone: the way dry-stone walling follows the patterns of layering in the bare terraces; the 'found stones' and vernacular gargoyles that adorn so many cottage walls and roofs.

This is a landscape where the human presence has been sympathetic towards local quirks and savours. These days most human manipulation of natural features involves a deliberate ironing-out of local identity and diversity for the sake of commercial convenience. Forestry plantations, CAP cash-crop fields, new golf courses, are as characterless as international airports. Off-the-peg ornamental trees – Japanese double-flowering cherries, robinias, black alders – are giving a uniform, garden festival look to towns across the land that maybe once sported indigenous willows and whitebeams. Even conservation policies, with the very best of intentions, can lead to a levelling out. Britain's hedges, for instance, a wonderfully diverse legacy, are declining and disappearing, and it is good that there are government-backed schemes to regenerate them. But the hedgerow revival has been accompanied by an indiscriminate zeal for management for its own sake, and tall Exmoor beech windbreaks, Suffolk ancient wood remnants and thick Dorset double-rows are all being beaten down to the level and scale of Midland quicksets.

But maybe I am being a killjoy. Isn't a regimented living hedge better than a vanished local speciality? Aren't street robinias brighter and more resilient than pollarded willows? Mightn't a commitment to local distinctiveness be difficult to disentangle from high-handed puritanism, or isolation, or even an unpleasant xenophobia (as in the recent pogrom against escaped American ruddy ducks)?

Earlier this year I was driving back from Shropshire on the first warm day of March, and all the way through the Long Mynd hills pairs of buzzards were spiralling in courtship displays on the thermals. As soon as I was down on the Midland plain, they were gone. I marvelled at what an extraordinary thing the buzzard line is, stretching as it does from Dorset through the Cotswolds and the eastern Lakes, even dividing lowland Scotland in two; and how entering buzzard country, and seeing those meditative, soaring shapes above the hills, is a sure sign of having crossed into the west. Then I remembered that this is an entirely unnatural state for the bird, which a century-and-a-half ago, before persecution by the game lobby, had been common throughout Britain. Its current restricted distribution, as flavoursome a westerly thing as cider or chapels, is, like that of the wild daffodil, an indication of unnatural depletion as much as local distinctiveness.

And as Dutch elm disease got a grip again this spring, I thought about its victims, whose story is another salutary if ambivalent parable. Elms are one of the most locally diverse of all our native trees. Different types, reproducing largely by suckers, have evolved in different parts of Britain: stiff, fastigiate kinds, twiggy kinds, varieties with an almost black bark, and an all but infinite variety of leaf shapes to match; and some, like the Boxworth elm of the country round Huntingdon, more or less resistant to the disease. The great elm specialist Professor R. H. Richens found that there was a distinctive elm type in almost every East Anglian valley. The local trees, isolated genetically from those in the next valley, were the source of the cuttings and suckers used to make the local hedges, which after a while formed a treescape subtly different from that in the next village. Ironically, the human inhabitants were probably quite unaware of these botanical differences; and though the genetic variety of the nation's elms is part of the species' insurance policy, the cloning of local varieties means that if any one tree in a village catches the disease all will likely go under. Local distinctiveness in terms of natural resources, pursued too narrowly, can represent a dead end, a state of siege as much as an oasis.

The fenlands of East Anglia are an extreme example of a distinctive locality which has become an impoverished landscape for all its life forms. It is still a place with a powerful aura, determined by the huge imperatives of sky, wind and water. Yet most of its old liveliness has been drained and sprayed into oblivion, and it has become a place of sad paradoxes. I have seen scores of black-dressed women hunched over the potato crop like a vision of the worst times of the nineteenth-century agricultural depression. And a few hundred yards away, signs warning passers-by to stay off the fields because of the 'deadly poisons'.

People living on the edge of the Fens have an inexhaustible supply of slanderous stories about the inhabitants of this drained swamp, inland from the Wash. They are, the myths go, insular, inbred and violent – 'Fen Tigers'. They work their children as slave labour in the fields. They are so greedy that they plough up to the very edge of the drainage dykes, and are forever falling off their tractors and drowning themselves. The Fens are eastern England's Balkans. Every stereotype that has been glimpsed in, or fabricated about, the rural population at large has been magnified and dumped on this vast plain of fertile peat. Even the landscape itself, a grid of featureless flat rectangles clear to the horizon, can seem like a bleak caricature of the modern farmscape.

The unusual thing is that the local people themselves don't dispute many of these images. They are acutely aware of the brutalising effects of centuries of isolation, of the ceaseless battle against flooding, and of the corrosive influence of modern agriculture. In the nineteenth century, rheumatism and 'the ague' were endemic, and opium use was common well into the 1920s. Today it is depression and drink, and 'fen syndrome', described by psychiatrists as a kind of 'cultural retardation', is a matter of medical record in the region.

But people have loved and still love this place. The poet John Clare did, even after the first stages of its enforced enclosure and modernisation had helped drive him mad. It is a measure of just how vital locality is to us that we cling to, and can get comfort from, the slightest shadows and echoes of the old spirit of a place.

The challenge, in a world where the differences between native and stranger are fading, is to discover veins of local character which are distinctive without being insular and withdrawn.

1993

What Shapes a View?

What shapes a view? '*Who* shaped a view?' is a more usual question, so drummed into us has been the idea that the English countryside is an entirely human creation, a monument to generations of wise husbandry and a three-dimensional landscape painting rolled into one.

Driving along this stretch of the Chiltern scarp, through a tunnel of riotous hazel and hornbeam that just occasionally permits a peep at the next peninsula of ragged woodland jutting out into the Vale of Aylesbury, I've sometimes laughed out loud at the sheer audacity of this belief. The view as pure artefact? From up here the distant fields look no more than inconsequential doodlings on an immense and bristling green pelt.

I drive on. The frame formed by the next gap in the hedge contains one huge arable field, and I realise I am guilty of generalisation myself. All kinds of forces have shaped these prospects, including – without becoming too philosophical – *my* point of view. Which straightaway brings to mind another question: does the view shape the viewer?

This road has been an education. It links the town where I live with the next-door village of Wigginton where I bought a small wood nearly ten years ago, and I have been travelling along it two or three times a week ever since. Part of it follows the route of a neolithic ridgeway and even in three short miles you have a sense of history rolling back. You leave the executive villas behind, pass through a belt of nineteenth-century arable enclosures, and begin to drop down through a maze of deep medieval banks and ditches. To your right is the edge of the Aylesbury Vale, one of the few points where water has breached the Chilterns' western redoubts; and beyond that the plateau of Berkhamsted Common, where one of the great battles against Enclosure was won in 1866.

Then, when the lane has burrowed almost to the valley bottom, it splits in two, and corkscrews round through nearly 150 degrees to begin climbing back – due south, into the hill country. From here I can just see my patch – Hardings Wood – squatting close to the top of the hill, a green tump with an oddly abrupt edge that was obviously once destined for bigger things. The wood is nearly 700 feet up, and in all senses in a different climate from the valley. The land around it is deceptively tame: paddocks, hobby farms, some shrinking stretches of grass and barley. There are few footpaths, no common land, clusters of neat Rothschild estate cottages, and a very straight road leading to the village centre. But inside the wood there are intimations of something more turbulent. It straddles a V-shaped valley, sharp enough to make you feel there should be a stream there. Perhaps there was once. These Chiltern side-valleys and shallow combes were carved out by long-vanished watercourses and glaciers. If I lean on the gate at the foot of the wood and look back along the lane I climbed up from the valley, the landscape has a worn, parched air behind the curtains of green. There are tangles of old man's beard and whitebeam, flashes of white under the hedges where badgers have dug down through the clay to the chalk below.

Geology has been a persistent influence here, a constraint and an opportunity. Following the combe bottom is a mysterious earthwork called Grim's Ditch, bits of which are scattered throughout the Chilterns. There is no firm evidence about when it was dug, so people explain its origins according to their own historical preferences. It has been a Celtic ranch boundary, a Roman fortification, a Saxon estate marker. Whatever its beginnings there is an even chance it was built by slave labour. (Early this century,

73

when the wood was first sold off separately from the surrounding farmland, families living in cottages nearby were given the right to drain sewage into it – down the Ditch and into the bluebells.)

Between the 1750s and 1850s Wigginton parish was transformed by a massive programme of 'improvement'. On a map of 1766 the parish is shown as almost completely covered by commonland and wood. But by the early years of the eighteenth century two-thirds of the woodland has vanished, leaving just five little island copses (of which Hardings is one) amongst the new fields. There is no record of exactly why this clearance happened, but little doubt about who was responsible.

The Harcourt family, Lords of the Manor, confirmed their ambition a few years later, when they petitioned for the Enclosure of Wigginton's 300 acres of common. I have read the minutes of the meetings the twenty-four local landowners held with the surveyor during the early months of 1853. They met in the Royal Hotel, Tring, about a dozen of them at a time, and systematically replanned the home country of 629 people. It says so much, that meticulously penned address on top of the quarto sheets. The Royal was a commercial inn, outside the village, right next to Tring railway station and convenient for agents and absentee owners. Here, over lunch, they argued about how much of the common each of them should be allotted and set down the reasons for Enclosure: 'increased productiveness of the land, useful employment of labour . . . and improvement in the morals and habits of the people'. And on 7 August they agreed their plan for reorganising the parish's communication system. Two weeks later the posters, printed in heavy block type, like 'Wanted' notices, went up all over the village. Thirteen existing ways and footpaths were to be completely closed, and replaced by two surveyor's roads leading to the nearby towns. One of the footpaths stopped off was a track leading from Wigginton Village to the valley, which passed through Hardings Wood. Not the slightest evidence that it ever existed remains.

By the end of the year the Enclosure was complete. The fences had been raised and the commoners and landless poor of Wigginton had been left with a two-acre recreation field and five acres of allotment. Even by the standards of Parliamentary Enclosure it was a callous act, and it is odd that the people of the village did not resist (as they had, fiercely, against an earlier attempt at enclosure).

In the following year, 1854, the new curate at Wigginton – by no means a radical – set down some revealing comments on the consequences of the Enclosure Award:

> All the picturesque appearance of the place was gone, and
> perhaps the poetry. Post and rail fences were right and left all
> over the place. But I believed that the change would morally
> tend to the benefit of the people: they would be less rough,
> wild and uncivilised. I cannot judge whether this has happened;
> whether as some predicted 'wicked Wigginton would become
> virtuous Wigginton'. I cannot say that the people as I knew
> them deserved the former epithet, or differed very much from
> other people of whom I have experience. But as I look back I
> am much surprised that they accepted the enclosure as patiently as
> they did, considering of how many rights the enclosure deprived
> them.

The irony is that not a hint of the harshness of these events remains in the landscape itself, no sense of hurt or reproof; just, in winter sometimes, the slightest feeling of over-orderliness, of a loss of breathing-space in the hard geometry of the fields. But at all other times it seems to be in a state of grace, to be making a continual gesture of reparation. Grim's Ditch, despite its murky past, always carries the first flowers of spring, a pale glimmer of celandine and moschatel on the dark banks. What were once the old post and rail fences are now hedges covered by wild roses; and along the Enclosure road the verges are thick with self-sown oak trees.

Yet this magnanimous flooding back of life has happened in spite of those bitter events of 1853, not because of them. To claim human credit for this landscape is a little like boasting about an old war wound. There is a fading reminder of the pain and conflict; but the healing has all been, as it were, *against* the wound. When I think of what gives this view its real character and texture – the wonderful switchback contours of the ground, the bluebells that flood the wood every May, the flints that wash down into the lane after August storms, that ceaseless press by woods and hedges to reclaim the fields wrenched from them – there isn't a single man-made feature amongst them. We create (sometimes) sensible and sensitive scaffoldings for the landscape; but the life and colour that fills the view is, thank goodness, something that transcends our skill.

1989

A Chiltern Ramble

I'd glimpsed the gibbet beech just before I parked the car. It arched over the road, its branches hung with pallid and eviscerated forms. I walked back towards it in a state of foreboding, expecting to see a tree full of stretched squirrels, the latest band of martyrs in the local foresters' pogrom. It wasn't until I was directly underneath that I saw they were pairs of discarded trainers, chucked into the twiggery like *bolas*, and now walking on air. Of course! This was the Chilterns after all, a quirky, secretive landscape where there are arcane carvings in the chalk and the occasional escaped emu in the lanes.

I've lived in and walked obsessively round my own patch of the central Chilterns for much of my life, and that kind of familiarity can breed complacency, a habitual way of looking. I had long had the fancy of breaking the pattern, of walking free-range in the southern reaches of the hills, of following my nose in Coleridge's 'mazy motion' rather than a pre-ordained route – and a shoe-tree seemed a rather auspicious omen for the task.

It was blustery April weather when I set off south from Kingston Blount along the Ridgeway. The old track isn't strictly a ridge-way here; it follows the erratic western edge of the scarp on a contour that is usually about 300 feet from the top. But it's as wide as a cricket pitch, and on that day mightily exposed to the south-westerly winds sweeping over the Oxford plain.

77

I was soon following a rather doggish route, swinging from one side of the track to the other to escape the gusts, peer at a flower or scan the woods to the east. They straggle down the hill here, beechwoods edged with yew and ash, and with only fenced farmland to stop them ramping all the way to the valley. Along the foot of Aston Rowant National Nature Reserve the thin strip of arable between wood and track vanishes altogether, to be replaced by downland and scrub. This is a much derided habitat, but is in fact just the early stages of natural woodland recolonisation. Here it is full-blown chalk scrub, a mixture of dogwood, spindle, old man's beard, maple, rose, a little juniper, and in autumn the massed colours, ranging from lemon to deepest plum, quite outshine the beech.

Occasionally the track passed through a straggling patch of trees, and, despite the chilling weather, the woodland ground flora was beginning to show. Dog violets, anemones and wood spurge were in flower, and the bright green leaf-whorls of wood-ruff already above ground. These are species that are regarded as indicators of long-established woodland, and showed how even green lanes and hedgebanks in anciently forested areas like this retain some kind of link with the wildwood.

The track tunnels right under the M40 here, in a bizarre conjunction between neolithic and twentieth-century transport routes. From the far end of the underpass I could see the immense gulch the motorway had created when it was blasted through Beacon Hill. But the road itself was invisible, and the gap had the incongruous look of a cutting made by a river or glacier. It was not hard to imagine it filling with undergrowth again in a saner future.

A mile further on, I was tempted off the Ridgeway. To my left lay Shirburn Hill, looking for all the world like a wild sweep of *maquis* in southern France. Ragged tongues of yew slewed up the hill, alongside sunken tracks full of tangled rose and ivy. There were lines of hulking beech pollards, and hornbeams that may have once been part of a layered hedge but which were now so arthritically twisted and gale-bent that their ancient lower branches had struck into the ground and emerged a few yards further on, as good as new saplings. Amongst them, to add to the southern feeling, was a half-wrecked cork oak.

But it was the box groves, sprawling hummocks of dark green clinging to the side of the hill, that fascinated me most. I climbed up the sheer slope towards them, over acres of grassland cloaked with moss and riddled with rabbit warrens and ant-hills. They were immense and pungent and quite impenetrable. They are quite likely native on these chalk slopes (as they certainly are just a mile north), but their natural compactness made them look as if they had been topiaried.

I pondered on the origins of this strange wooded pasture, which had the feel of a fallen landscape garden or a deer park abandoned to more lowly creatures, as I took the footpath up the hill. Sticking to my plan I allowed this happenstance diversion to decide my route – which now lay due east, up a dry chalk track by the edge of the Aston Rowant reserve. It was an exhilarating climb, through a mosaic of wood and downland chequerboarded in a classic Chiltern pattern: folds and grooves of grassland scalloped out of the woods; and neat strips of plantation wood struck back across the down.

I saw from the map that I was heading for Cowleaze Wood, which sounded intriguing – an old wooded common maybe. Sadly it had been covered by a Forestry Commission conifer plantation, but it is now the site of the Chiltern Sculpture Park, and for the next hour or so I meandered round a trail of greenwood fantasies and puns that kept reminding me of the plimsoll tree and the box groves.

The piece that struck me most of all lay in a wedge of land between two converging paths, and consisted of a long, gently curving wooden rib supported at about twelve feet above ground level on trestles. It was minimalist to a fault, but I am still working out the ways in which it affected me. At a purely visual level its thin, tentative – I am tempted to say pencilled – horizontal line emphasised how much woods are places of strong verticals, of shoots growing towards the light. Then the rib suddenly seemed like a walkway, tracing out the aerial paths of squirrels and mice; then, at a more practical level, I saw the rough trestle poles (cut from thinnings on the site) as reminders of a piece of local history – the Chiltern bodgers who used to work in the woods. Close by was a stranger, more challenging piece: the skeleton of a small tree welded out of iron and, in place of leaves, carrying a cast-iron fish at the end of each branch. While I was gazing up at it, a glider passed overhead, through the mesh of ferrous carp and lime-green larch shoots – a vision in three different elements. Another short walk brought me to a huge picnic table, eight feet high, with a painted blue-and-white check tablecloth. It was visible a hundred yards away, lurking amongst the pines, and was the best visual joke in the wood – acting as a shelter for having picnics *under*.

Sometimes I was not sure if I was looking at a deliberate work or a natural happening – which is exactly as it should be. Cowleaze is full of cryptic tunnels cut through the trees, and 'found logs' in clearings. And at the eastern tip of the trail there is a view over the Ibstone valley of another kind of sculpture park altogether. All along the south-west facing slopes, the woods were full of the white root-plates of gale-strewn beeches, looking like a vast chalk henge. They were on the extensive and much barricaded Wormsley estate, but I found a footpath and turned south through the valley. Many of the beech trees in Bowleys Wood and Ibstone Common had been knocked over like skittles, a severe caution to all those foresters who have forced the Chilterns towards single-species plantations of this shallow-rooted tree. The local woods were more mixed two centuries ago, and signs of the natural tree cover – ash, maple, yew, cherry – were already beginning to spring up in the bare patches between the fallen beeches and whatever was inside the rows of plastic tree-shelters.

This is a region of marvellous sunken lanes, and I climbed towards Northend up a corkscrew track lined with gnarled maples and violets. The road east from Northend to Turville is, for my taste, the best in the Chilterns. It runs along a gently roller-coastering ridge for close on three miles, and is sunken all the way. The banks are a tumult of flints and twisted roots, topped with the bright green shoots of wood melick, and above them you catch sudden, continually changing views of the narrow side-valleys and coombes running down to Ibstone. With the light failing and rain beginning, I was happy to keep to the lanes for my last few miles to Hambleden.

The next day the weather is very bad, with streaming, chill rain and thickening mud on all the tracks. I stay in the lee of the hollow lanes wherever possible as I tack westwards to Fawley. There are unseasonal tit and chaffinch flocks and what I fear may be the new local game-crop, red-legged partridges, sheltering everywhere in the verges and wood edges. But on stiff uphill beats I am suffocating in my Gortex hood, which is contriving to trap the sickly-sweet smell of spring fungicides blowing from the barley fields. The strips of arable beyond the lanes and tucked between the woods increasingly seem like an irrelevant imposition on the place, and I begin to dream of the Chilterns reclaiming its old woodland and pasturage; of the return of bodgers and commoners and smallholders.

Coming down a steep drop into Fawley Bottom I find some relics of the old Chiltern economy. It is a patch of coppice wood – not that common here. There is hazel, maple, some oak, and what I take from the distance to be unusually straight and smooth-barked ashes. The stools are wide and multi-stemmed and probably last cut about forty years ago. But close to I see pink-flushed leaf buds studded on alternate sides along the twigs and realise that they are that very scarce and curious tree the large-leaved lime, a component of the ancient wildwood that is being discovered in many sites on the southern chalk hills. Perhaps this stand is a rare outlier or a planted population. Either way its coppice form is a reminder that the Chilterns' woodlands were once a more shared resource than now, providing not only local fuel-wood but much of London's, too.

I plod on further west, through more diverse kinds of wood, the wild expanses of Bix Bottom nature reserve at Maidensgrove – almost like a miniature New Forest – and the naturally regenerating

81

beechwoods below Nettlebed, finally arriving, aptly, at the Crooked Billet in Stoke Row. I suddenly realise, with a pang, that I could have pubcrawled as well as woodcrawled all the way here, through the Fox and Hounds at Christmas Common, the White Hart at Northend, the Bull and Butcher at Turville, the Fox at Bix – all small brick, flint and wood buildings that may once have been woodmen's inns. But the Crooked Billet is as good as any, a bosky cavern full of riotous woodery of all sorts – low beams, bric-a-brac, cranky unscrubbed tables, immense fires, jokes in logs; all rather like the Chilterns itself, where the best of human imprints in the landscape is like the well-worn seat of an old wooden chair.

1991

Living on the Edge

A PERFECT WEEKEND

My feeling is that the perfect weekend is the one that least resembles the end of the week. Perhaps it is my age or occupation. Certainly those who spend their weekdays in solitary freelance business seem more vulnerable to the emptiness and claustrophobia of the English Sunday, the dead phones, the great retreat into hermetically sealed family units. I can do without peace and quiet but not without company, conviviality, a little something unexpected and a lot of time out of doors.

If I was looking for a single word to describe my perfect weekend it would be 'tribal'. I should have left such longings behind in adolescence, and might have done so if they had not been irrevocably prolonged by Norfolk.

A friend had a converted lifeboat (called, inexplicably, *Dilemma X*) moored on the north Norfolk coast at Blakeney, and in my late teens groups of us used to wing our way there most weekends. *Dilemma*'s interior resembled a miniature prison hulk. It was a honeycomb of queer-shaped cavities and ballasted by yards of old railway line. The steering cabin sprouted all manner of inexplicable knobs and handles, and we never got to know the boat's full repertoire of night-time groanings and oleaginous smells.

Yet for the best part of a decade it served as our home

base while we played at being weekend bohemians, sleeping rough and dressing up like artists in smocks bought at the Great Grimsby Coal, Salt and Tanning Company in Sheringham. We bird-watched, gossiped, messed about in boats, but mostly just ran wild on those vast, exhilarating marshes that shelved and frayed so gently into the sea that they seemed to be almost illimitable.

I'm sure that the closeness of these edges of the land was crucial to those Norfolk weekends, reflecting our smug belief that we, too, were creatures of the fringelands. I spent a good deal of my time down on the mudflats, often sitting in something close to a trance as the first cord-grass stems bent in the changing current, the first perceptible new water oozed like a satin sheen across the mud and then burst in a thin rush between the rippled sandbanks until, astonishingly, whole square miles of apparently solid land had been transformed into sea. Hours later it emerged again, washed clean and with a new geography of islands and trenches and pools that had never existed exactly so before.

I said that one of the attractions of these weekends was their unpredictability, but on reflection this is not strictly true. In many ways they were highly ritualistic, a tireless round of pet customs and expeditions. Friday nights we spent in the local pub, Saturday mornings mooching about the quay. If the weather was fine we would go out to the long shingle spit called Blakeney Point and in high summer would spend whole days out there, lounging among the dunes.

Nothing ever happened. We dozed, played cricket with drift-wood bats and picked bunches of samphire for supper. Occasionally we would come back on the evening tide in *Dilemma*'s tender, a rhapsodical trip with the setting sun behind us and little terns diving for fish along the edges of the boat's wash. Usually, though, we would trudge the three miles back round the rim of Blakeney Harbour at low water. It was a slapstick, foot-testing hike through sweeps of sea lavender and silver wormwood and mud – deep, black, glistening, sucking mud with the consistency of Vaseline. We arrived back in the village draped with edible greenery and wearing our grime like a badge of identity.

For Saturday-evening drinking we struck inland to the little flint villages on the so-called 'Norfolk heights', a drive through an airy landscape of vast pale fields and tall hedges, to a night of darts and political debate.

That pattern seemed peerless at the time, but in retrospect it had a kind of doggedness, a curiously rigid view of the perils of bourgeois civilisation. It was some time before any of us gave much thought to the human history of the landscape we used so cavalierly. The boat and the raw natural life of the marshes seemed a much more direct line to the heroic ideals of noble savagery to which we aspired.

But there was – at least in our terms – one absolutely perfect weekend. It was late July, and a hot sea breeze was blowing. A halcyon weekend – except that when we arrived at the quay we found that *Dilemma* had been beached for repainting, and was now perched at an angle of sixty degrees at the edge of the car park. It was a disagreeable shock for a while, but it didn't take us long to realise that our dream of being a conspicuous Utopian island slap in the middle of mainstream holidaying England had been perfectly realised. We ate our Sunday lunch (samphire and roast chicken, I remember – a perfect compromise) draped about the sloping deck, in full view of the day-trippers. We were about as comfortable as beached squid, but as happy as sandboys.

1987

THE WASH

The tidal reaches of the Wash, a vast and beguilingly flat expanse of sand, have a long history as levellers of ambition. In 1216, as every schoolboy knows, King John lost his treasure here. The royal baggage train set out from what was then the coastal village of Walpole St Andrew, got caught in the quicksands and sank without trace. From the early seventeenth century to the end of the eighteenth, encouraged by the success of Cornelius Vermuyden's schemes just inland in the Fens, farmers began draining marshlands all around the Wash's perimeter. They enclosed each successive wave of newly won land with massive embankments, sometimes topping them with thatch for extra strength, so that by the end of the eighteenth century the coastline and its settlements had moved nearly six miles north-east. Holbeach alone spawned five satellite villages to seaward, each one bearing the prefix of its mother-village.

Then the great drainage adventure petered out. Victorian entrepreneurs were ruined trying to edge still further into the delta. And in the terrible surge floods of 1953 the sea broke through the sea-defences and briefly reclaimed some of its ancestral territory. But by the technologically optimistic 1960s and 1970s many new Utopian schemes were floated for the Wash: it would become the site of London's third airport, built on a vast artificial island; or perhaps a whole new city; or maybe a giant reservoir with a barrage slung across its mouth. Like most earlier dreams, they foundered on the Wash's shifting sands.

Just about the only scenario which hasn't been suggested for this haunt of sirens (rather surprisingly, given its embattled history and wild aspect) is that it should become some kind of national park or statutory beauty spot. As a result the Wash has been spared the perennial arguments about whose needs should determine a landscape's identity: workers and residents, or viewers and visitors? The Wash simply isn't 'landscape' in the accepted sense. It is stark, dangerous, flat and devoid of topographical features. It isn't even land so much as a fugitive hybrid between earth and water. When the tide is swirling in over the corrugations in the sand it has the look more of oil than sea. Prospects here are refractive, hallucinatory. Winter fogs form a bowl in which there is no seam between sky and land, and nothing more than a rhythmic hiss to tell you where the sea lies. On clear days in summer the Wash becomes a place of mirages: lines of white coastal cottages, Hunstanton's cliffs, even the Boston Stump, seem to float above the horizon.

But the tangible landscapes of the Wash are more intimate and urgent: a shifting labyrinth of deep creeks that can fill with water in minutes, of black sucking mud cloaked with a deceptive silk sheen of algae, of water that can seem to move in all directions at once. They turn all visitors into hunter-gatherers, and make nonsense of that philosophical squabble between the local and the offcomer.

The Wash's profile, squared off by centuries of land reclamation, disguises the fact that it is an estuary. Half of middle-England drains into it down the Welland, Ouse and Nene rivers. And with the water comes immense quantities of silt, which combines with seaborne matter to create a hundred square miles of biologically teeming mudflats. Herds of grey and common seals fish, breed and sunbathe on the sandbanks. The second largest concentration of wading birds in Britain – 180,000 mixed knot, dunlin, redshank, curlew and oystercatcher – catch crustaceans, insects and worms. So do the few humans who make a livelihood here. 'Strand-loopers' still dig for cockles and lugworms (for the Midland angling market) and share in the strange ambivalence of this amphibious world. They map the sands in the language of landworkers, talking of hills, valleys and ditches, and giving to the biggest flats names which could have come straight from an inland fieldscape: Puff, Mare's Tail, The Scalp. I have seen diggers going onto the sands with ponies and carts, sleds, even curious tyre-less bicycles. All of them know that the tide here comes in faster than a person can walk. Nothing survives here unless it respects the imperatives of weather and geography.

Patrick Sutherland's photographs capture this austere discipline. The figures in his landscapes don't gaze out expansively over distant prospects. They look down for their footing, focus intently on distant birds or the movement of the water. Local wildfowlers and visiting wader-ringers suffer the cold equally. MoD practice targets (like all wastes, the Wash has proved a magnet for the military) look like worm-eaten wrecks, and unexploded shells take on the form of fish. And Ron Fisher, mussel-gatherer, slithers towards his next net. It is a picture full of tension and uncertainty. His head is down, his catch being dragged urgently behind him. The mudflats are oozing water, the tide may be turning, the muddled valleys between the sand-ridges seem to have no obvious pattern.

This is a landscape defined neither by local appropriation nor distant aesthetics, but by hard-won familiarity.

1991

The Severn Estuary

The Severn is not quite like other English rivers. You wouldn't think of lounging in a punt in it, or playing Poohsticks under the bridges. It is dramatic, unpredictable, rumbustious, as far from a willow-lined brook as you can imagine. It is an *epic* river, the longest in Britain, taking in two nations, half the West Country, and hundreds of square miles of hectic water.

Or, rather, part of it is. For three-quarters of its 220 miles the Severn is a sedate mirror image of the Thames, meandering along the border country, through Upton upon Severn and Stourport on Severn and under the seventeenth-century bridge at Atcham, until it vanishes into its watersheds on Plynlimon – a river only really known to those who live near it. For the rest of us the Severn is synonymous with its estuary, an unruly snake of water that begins just below Gloucester and, after one elegant ox-bow around Arlingham, surges out to the Atlantic on a front that is never less than a mile wide.

This is the stretch that gives its name to things other than quiet villages on the Marches. This is where Severn salmon still run against a ferocious tide-race and a gauntlet of wicker traps which are probably prehistoric in design; where there is a miniature island fortress (Steepholm) that has in its time been a medieval monastic herb farm and a Victorian gun battery; and where the biggest bridge in Britain stands so high above the water that traffic is regularly banned from it when the wind is up. It is the route, most memorably, of the Severn Bore, a wall of tidal water created by the river's sharply funnelled profile that sometimes charges upstream furiously enough for surfers to ride it all the way from Newnham to Gloucester. And in a nod of acknowledgement to the sluicing power of its tides, it supports a vast concentration of industrial development at Avonmouth, and no less than four nuclear power stations. It is teeming, diverse, energetic, and no one would dream of calling it Old Father Severn.

When I was at school and drawing the outline of Britain from memory was a regular chore, we were always told to imagine the Severn as the nation's mouth. Looking at a map now this seems more like a metaphor than a memory jog. The estuary is an immense rictus, already twelve miles wide at its notional entrance between Nash and Harlestone Points. By rights it ought to have become the national maw, luring in every adventurous colonist and trader and shifting our centre of economic gravity over to the west. This is surely one of our more tantalising historical 'what-ifs': what if sassy, extrovert Bristol had become the capital of the UK? Or Cardiff, for that matter?

What stopped it was the Severn mud, which is as mobile and temperamental as its water. At low tide the river shrinks to a quarter of its full width, and the estuary becomes an outsized creek, with a sinister fretwork of dark rock shoals and sand spits.

During the spring high tides, when the water slaps up close to the rim of the flood defence banks, it can swing to the opposite extreme. My first glimpses of the estuary, like that of most visitors, I suspect, were from way up on the Severn Bridge, and then, glinting beyond the trees, from the Forest of Dean. On both occasions it seemed too vast and distant to be a river. It had the feel of a delta system, or an inland sea. When I went bird-watching in Bridgewater Bay, where the estuary is nearly twenty miles wide, it became a geographical abstraction, an idea which lumped together a host of idiosyncratic local landscapes that had no connection other than their closeness to this mass of incoherent water.

Even when I had one of those concentrated but casual writer's intimacies with a Severnside village in the mid-1980s, the estuary's image scarcely became any sharper. A cache of Victorian flower paintings had been discovered in the attic of the Clifford family's house in Frampton on Severn, and I'd been given the job of editing them into book form. The Cliffords have lived in Frampton since the days of William the Conqueror, and, give or take a few floodings, minor court scandals and bouts of heirlessness, have had a long and harmonious relation with the estuary. Between 1837 and 1850 six of their sisters and aunts, mostly unmarried, painted a remarkable group portfolio of the wild flowers of the neighbourhood. Yet the estuary itself, which must have been the dominant feature of their home landscape, gets a mere half-dozen species into the collection.

Down along these southern margins of the estuary it still seems as if the river is held at arm's length. Cattle follow medieval green lanes down to grasslands that owe at least part of their luxuriance to past flooding and silting. But that is about the only concession that is made to the river, and the fields are now drained and cultivated right up to the sea-walls. And though elvers – the young eels that migrate in astronomical numbers up the Severn in March and April – are still caught in cheesecloth nets (and gobbled in competitions on Frampton Green), most of the harvests here are not from the river itself, but from the legacies it has laid down over the millennia. Gravel is quarried in the vale, coal and iron ore mined up in the Forest of Dean. A soapy blue clay that lies under parts of the river and in exposures in the cliffs is still dug for bricks. The wall round the Victorian garden at Frampton Court is built from them, and weeps salt on hot days.

Now there is another crop on the horizon. The raw energy of the river, which was ultimately responsible for all these products, is itself being sized up as a possible harvest, and not for the first time in its history the Severn estuary is deeply immersed in a controversy about where we should draw the boundary between nature and culture.

There have been dreams of a barrage across the estuary since the 1930s, but the current scheme, supported by the Department of Energy, has got as far as a working model and feasibility and impact studies. It envisages a string of turbines ten miles long between Lavernock Point on the Welsh side and Brean Down on the English. The projected cost had already passed six billion pounds by the end of 1988, and it is reckoned that the electricity it would produce would be notionally at least twice as expensive as that from coal-fired or nuclear power stations. Yet it remains a tempting vision, the harnessing of this great cauldron of natural, renewable energy, and the provision perhaps of a clean and safe alternative to what may become the estuary's *fifth* nuclear power station – the proposed PWR at Hinkley Point.

The barrage would close and generate power only on the ebb tide, and would roughly halve the current tidal range between high and low water. So at low tide the estuary would be in much the same state as it presently is at mid-tide. There's little doubt that the project is viable, and that it could contribute between 2.5 and 5 per cent of the nation's need. But its likely ecological and social impacts have still barely been charted.

With the area of low-tide, food-rich mud reduced by a half, what would happen to the huge flocks of wading birds for which the estuary has been declared a Special Protection Area under the European Commission Bird Directive? Would the Bore become a ripple? Would spring salmon, having swum thousands of miles to reach their spawning grounds, be unable to get out to sea again? Worse, would the effluent from Avonmouth – already a potent cocktail of toxic metals and sewage – also be dammed in? Reducing the Severn estuary to a meek and rancid pond would be an ironic price to pay for our first large-scale project in alternative energy. For huge and diverse though it may be, the Severn does have a character all of its own.

I had a belated taste of this during my sojourn at Frampton. It was a hot day in high summer, and Rollo and Janie Clifford, their four children and I decided to go for a picnic by the river. We set out on a bevy of ancient bicycles, along the flat lanes that etch the country south of the estuary. The air was hot and still between the high hedges and musky with meadowsweet and willow-herb, and we guzzled home-made elder-flower cordial. We had the road to ourselves. We freewheeled and sang and spotted a pure white sparrow. It felt absurdly like a Famous Five expedition from the 1930s. But of the Severn there was not a sign. Then we swung into the field where we were to have our picnic, and suddenly there was the immense openness of the estuary not a hundred yards away, with what felt like a gale funnelling in from the Atlantic. We cowered on the cliff top, pegged the picnic down with stones, and watched the wind rattling the salmon weather vane on the top of Framilode church. Ten miles downstream we could see the grey bulk of Berkeley nuclear power station, and, exactly opposite it, the Forest of Dean, with its Celtic temples and medieval mines. The two miles of white horses between them looked unnavigable, even under the baking July sun.

Then the tide went out and the river all but vanished. We clambered down the cliff and squelched our way through the claggy blue-grey mud. The children smothered themselves with muddy war paint and the rest of us treasure-hunted under the cliffs. They were spongy and insubstantial, a precarious wreckage of landslips, fossils, washed-out trees and flotsam, and we kept a nervous eye on the state of the river even though the tide wasn't due for hours. Rollo told me that when the local fishermen wade out at low water to put up their salmon basket-traps, they always wear two watches, just in case one stops. Standing in the Severn's slippery foundations that afternoon it was not difficult to under-stand why Bristol declined as a port once its slave traffic had been outlawed. The muddy Avon Gorge that joins it to the Severn remained an obstacle to heavy shipping until it was circumvented by the new docks at Avonmouth.

The Severn is classic borderland. But it is nothing like the estuaries of East Anglia, say, where much of the territory is an unresolved no-man's-land between earth and water. Here, quite unequivocally, there is the river, and there is the land; and the plough-ridges that stretch right up to the massive sea-defences show that things have gone about as far as they can in the business of turning one into the other.

What we glimpsed that afternoon on the cliff, a motif of cultivated landscapes cheek by jowl with wild water, is repeated with local variations all the way along the upper reaches of the estuary. To find Awre, the very first settlement on the north bank, you must burrow down through a network of hollow lanes with a ferny, almost West Country luxuriance. The village itself is a cluster of houses around a soaring riverside church, and was the starting point for a ferry which used to run Dean charcoal over to Frampton. At Aust, you can sit under the flickering shadows of the evening rush hour on the Severn Bridge and watch the dunlin flocks (the estuary holds 50,000 of this species in winter – nearly a fortieth of the world population) on their downstream fly-past to roost.

Between these two villages, along the southern side of the estuary, is a landscape of small fields and orchards and straggly hedges full of pollard ashes. It is one of the few places in England where pollards are still regularly cut for firewood, each tree about once every ten years, and the pale ends of the freshly lopped and stacked branches gleam behind the hedges.

Amidst these pastoral prospects you catch bizarre glimpses of the estuary's other human landscapes. A dip in the road and the hi-tech docks at Sharpness rear up momentarily between two barns. Oldbury nuclear power station is framed by garlands of pear-tree mistletoe.

Yet one is still never quite prepared for the first sight of Avonmouth. As you drive south from the Severn Bridge, the skyline begins to fill with cooling towers and gasholders, wreathed in pale orange smoke. This chemical metropolis now covers close on ten square miles. Most of the big multinationals are there and the effluent that consequently pours into the Severn is one of the most concentrated mixtures of pollutants in any British estuary. When I was last there one February, I saw one of the discharge pipes spraying effluent straight onto bare low-tide mud. Yet with a contrariness that is typical of Severnside, as I was panning the binoculars away from the pipe onto the tussocky waste ground that sits between Avonmouth and the river a patch of brown detritus

94

appeared to lift clear of the ground and float towards me. It was a short-eared owl, its huge tiger-yellow eyes glaring full ahead. It sheared off when it was about ten yards away, and I watched it circle over Severn Beach's caravan site, past the pub garden and the new holiday flats development, its plumage now a chequer of bluff and chestnut in the evening sun.

Even at Slimbridge, where The Wildfowl & Wetlands Trust's famous reserve gives an almost unseemly devotion to birds' comfort, these odd conjunctions continue. The shallow bay between Slimbridge village and the Severn is one of the last patches of real marshland on the estuary, and was a haven for waterbirds long before Sir Peter Scott rented it in 1946. Now it is probably the most civilised bird observatory in the world. There are hides sponsored by banks and binocular firms, admonitory and educational hides ('Remember, geese have ears'), double-storeyed, picture-windowed and centrally-heated hides. From them you can gaze out over a teeming landscape in which it is difficult to separate the wild and the tame. Swarms of geese mill about in the lakes, the pinioned exotics tempting in the wild migrants. Bewick swans commute between the wet meadows and the feeding pens. And on the extreme edge of the reserve, knot and dunlin flocks swirl about like a denser kind of smoke in front of the plumes rising up from the Welsh factories over the river.

This cheerfully promiscuous atmosphere is a powerful generator of confidence, in birds and humans alike. That February day there were coaches of children down from South Wales and the Midlands, and many and various were the sightings of Slimbridge's famous peregrines (wintering birds and occasional residents patrolling south from the Symonds Yat eyrie) recorded with shaky pencils in the hide log books: 'Falcon in bush.' 'Peregrine sitting in field near cow.' Some were no doubt wish-fulfilment falcons, but it is good that places exist where children from the Valleys can have such flights of the imagination.

Certainly the estuary looks a very different place from the Welsh side. England is barely visible through the spray when a Bore is brewing up. The decline of the coal and steel industries has left a ribbon of dereliction from Chepstow to Barry, a bleak landscape of corrugated-iron fencing, gappy hedges, rusting factories and sour paddocks, in which the countryside seems as blighted as the towns. The elegant port office at Penarth is now a hostel for the homeless, and that splendid example of Severnside ingenuity, the Newport transporter bridge, seems to spend most of its time under repair. The bridge is an exquisitely engineered solution to the problem of getting cars over the River Usk at its junction with the Severn. It carries vehicles and passengers in a carriage slung under a moving trolley, cable-car fashion. Now, with no ships needing the headroom it was designed to provide, it has become an anachronism.

There are schemes to rejuvenate the Welsh side of the estuary, and the burgeoning leisure and technology parks do at least carry something of the optimism that transformed Swansea a decade ago. But the most ambitious scheme, to turn Cardiff Bay into a huge lake by means of a mile-long barrage, is a well-meaning but shortsighted attempt to create a Docklands-style development in a totally different context. Building the complex of offices, restaurants and marinas will provide thousands of temporary jobs in an area of severe unemployment, but it will mean the end for 8,000 wading birds that spend the winter in part of what is now internationally recognised as the Severn Special Protection Area. And in place of the decaying but distinctive character of old Cardiff will come the anonymous glitz of International Maritime, the style of the times.

The Cardiff Bay scheme may provide a foretaste of the impact of the Severn Barrage itself, and be the first step in the transformation of the estuary into a giant *Howard's Way* set. It's a prospect which rather tickles the fancy of some of the villagers along the Gloucester shore, who foresee their property values soaring.

Barrages of all kinds are fashionable at present, but they are nothing new. Up in the Forest of Dean they have been fighting attempts to level out the region's character and quirkiness for a thousand years. Dean, properly speaking, is not part of the estuary, but it has had a long symbiotic relationship with it, and Lydney was once an important port for off-loading coal, iron ore and timber from the Forest. But ever since the Normans declared Dean a royal hunting preserve, there have been attempts by powerful outside interests to expropriate its natural wealth. In the early sixteenth century it was big ironmasters such as Sir John de Winter; later that century, the Navy. In 1831 the enclosure of the forest by the Commissioner of Woods and Forests led to a wholesale local uprising. Every one of these cases was an attempt to deprive the local people of their ancient and vastly complex network of common rights. But on each occasion commoners, Free Miners and 'ship badgers' (sheep keepers) fought back, and as a result Dean has retained a local distinctiveness that is probably unique in southern England.

The sixth-century temple that looks out over the estuary from just inside the Forest at Lydbrook is dedicated to Nodens, a god of healing who also took care of the river. The temple is decorated with fish and sea-monsters, and was almost certainly the work of Romanised Celts. So far, the Severn Barrage, benign in intention but remorselessly authoritarian in its likely effects, is a very Roman-looking idea. What is needed now is some input from the Celtic tradition, with its love of ingenuity and ornamentation and its fierce tribal respect of the spirit of place.

1989

A Limestone Landscape

Landscapes are supposed to be cut down to size on second visits, to lose their sense of holding something back. Not so the Burren in County Clare, which, for me at least, has swelled to sublime proportions over the years.

I first visited this 400-square-kilometre expanse of shattered limestone in the mid-1970s. There were four of us on the trip, all mad for flowers, and we spent that June week in a kind of myopic ecstasy, riveted by the magic and sheer Irishness of every incongruous bloom and crevice. On the shores of Galway Bay, we scraped sea-salt crystals from the beds of spongy, lichen-blacked limestone that dip down into the Atlantic. In Lisdoonvarna, a town of shrines and spas, we lounged under palm trees in the languid air and watched the nuns parade past. But mostly we just peered in amazement at the flowers at our feet, at their brilliant profusion and contempt for botanical protocol. Spring gentians grew next to sea-pinks; mountain avens – tufts of pure-white petals and twisted, silky seed-plumes – were more luxuriant than the grass; and there were centuries-old trees, rooted in the deep fissures in the rock, that had never reached above ground level. I remember wearing through a brand-new pair of fashionable Kickers hopping about the razorbacked crags – an achievement which sums up rather well my naive passion for the place. I saw all the bejewelled fragments, but barely noticed the immense geological story written in the rocks, or the evidence of at least 4,000 years of human occupation.

When I went back to the Burren last July, fifteen years older and not quite so single-minded, it seemed impossibly vast. As so often in this place of incongruity and optical illusion, serendipity played a part in broadening my outlook. I had been driving up from Shannon airport, through miles of that archetypal Celtic fieldscape of straggly blackthorn hedges and rushy pastures dotted with little round haycocks. Then, somewhere north of Lisdoonvarna, I got tangled up with a herd of homebound cattle on a steep downhill road. We spiralled along the narrow S-bends together at a graceful, glacial pace; and through the melee of Friesian necks and roadside trees I caught my first glimpse of the Moneen hills rotating gently the other way – as white as bleached bone, and like a bright new island rising out of the green valley-lands.

I had the same view, only closer, from my hotel in Gragan. It was a classic Burren vista: a series of hunched limestone ridges, receding into the distance. That evening I sat by my window and watched the rocks pick up first the golds, then the pinks of the sunset; and then, as the light faded, show every glaciated shelf and terrace in silhouette.

The Burren is named from the Celtic *boirrean*, a stony place. There are tracts of sour shale and moorland, but it is exposed limestone that dominates the landscape and gives it character and liveliness. Limestone has a stark and austere feel only in distant profile, and in every other way seems disarmingly open and adaptable. It wears its history on its sleeve – or maybe like lines on its face. In his strange, audacious poem 'In Praise of Limestone', W. H. Auden called it 'a stone that responds', an ice-sculpted, weatherworn rock that is marked out 'because it dissolves in water'. Almost all the typical features of the Burren landscape – the scree-strewn scars, the flattened terraces, the grooved 'pavements' – depend on this fact.

The Burren was even born this way, laid down under shallow seas 300 million years ago from the slow, skeletal rain of myriads of dead sea creatures. Later, earth movements raised and buckled the hills and sent searing splits through the rock layers, most of them running roughly north–south. (The splits are known as 'grikes' and the flat rock slabs between them as 'clints'.) Thousands of years of weathering scraped out the rough pattern of valleys, hills and terraces that are visible today. Finally, about 20,000 years ago, the glaciers of the last ice age rounded off the slopes, scoured the limestone bare in some places and dumped drifts of clay and gravel in others.

Seven thousand years ago the Burren almost certainly developed a scattered cover of open, deciduous woodland. Then, about 3,500 BC, the first farmers (probably from the Mediterranean) arrived with their crops and cattle. They found the light woodland, loosely rooted on soft rock, easy to clear, and grazing animals, heavy rainfall and soil erosion ensured that it didn't grow back. For the last few hundred years the Burren has been as open as it probably was soon after the retreat of the last glaciers.

Has the landscape helped shape the inhabitants, as well as being shaped by them? Auden reckoned these intricate regions of 'short distances and definite places' bred hedonistic, capricious characters. Certainly the Burren's history seems full of paradox and impulsiveness. It looks barren at first sight, but, well-drained and warmed by the Gulf Stream, stays green enough through winter for the local farmers to operate a system that is a converse of the continental tradition of transhumance. The stock are taken up into the hills in late autumn and down into the valley pastures in summer.

Yet despite this year-round fertility, occupation in the Burren seems to have been a transient and hard-won affair. The area is littered with the shells of dwellings and monuments from almost every period of history since the Bronze Age – all now tumbling back to rock. Even its basic ecology is baffling – an aggregation of plants that occur together nowhere else in Europe; Mediterranean and Arctic, mountain and seashore, woodland and field species sometimes grow in the same few square yards. How did they get here? Or is it more a question of why so few of them were driven away? About 10,000 years ago, before the climax forest was fully established, plants we now think of as confined to specialised habitats probably grew side by side throughout the dry part of Britain. The weather was benign, the ground open and unshaded and there was no great competition for space. Then – in eastern and northern Britain, at least – came climate change, the great shading by the wildwood, and the arrival of agriculture. Each one of these developments acted to drive the more sensitive species into marginal refuges.

But these traumatic changes were much less marked in the Burren. It has remained a congenial place, free of frost and flood and of dense woodland cover, and its remarkable flora may be an authentic relic of that post-glacial Eden.

Limestone seems to exert a congenial influence on me, too. For a whole day I ranged about the hills between Ballyvaughan and Kilnaboy, stopping the car at any likely crag or pavement and rock-hopping away. The bright – barefaced, you could say – intricacy of the rock seems to pull you up and along, niche-hunting like a migrant plant yourself.

At the foot of the hills the rock is usually tangled with low blackthorn scrub, drapes of bloody cranesbill (in full magenta flower in early July) and burnet roses, whose cream-coloured flowers fill the breeze with scent. You climb up, and every lip and crack of rock seems to be different – bevelled, rounded, honeycombed, leached by water, sometimes redeposited as stone wormcasts or imitation fossils: 'definite places' indeed. You spot a glossy hart's-tongue fern in a deep grike, grown enormously long in its search for the light; feathery sprays of meadow-rue; an ancient ash tree, extending horizontally along a crevice, and another topiaried by grazing animals into an almost perfect hemisphere.

Every so often the rocky hillsides flatten into plateaux, or into true limestone pavements which have been scoured of most of their turf. This is where the great mats of spring flowers grow, often on thick platforms of humus that have built upon the clints. It is also very sonorous landscape. Desiccated lichens and rose leaves crisped in the July sun scrunch underfoot; loose clints sway and clatter, a bony, ringing, almost tonic note. I hear a few words floating from the Tannoy of a sightseeing coach in the distance –

'400 years ago, the Burren . . .' I never hear the rest. The past here seems insubstantial, rock-dust, not much older than the seed heads of the gentian and orchid flowers that drench these plateaux blue, white and purple in May. The landscape seems fresh-minted, and in the glaring sun reflected off the white rock it has the look of an image emerging on a photographic plate. I am tugged this way and that by things just at the edge of vision: a pool of distant yellow which turns into a prostrate gold-leaved holly; a trompe-l'oeil wedge-tomb six inches high, which some walker had propped up on a slab. I need to make a conscious effort to stop and perch on a boulder. Even then the landscape still seems to be on the move. Flakes of mica-thin rock, limestone *millefeuille*, flutter down the terraces. The breeze ruffles a thin puddle of water on top of a slab – a 'tadpole runnel' that will eventually dissolve its way through the rock.

I look down over miles of terraces below me, and find it hard to believe that there was ever anything as monumental as a forest here. How long could a tree have lasted (even without human interference) with its roots twisted round this friable rock? Was the primeval woodland here not only full of glades and gaps, but feet-deep in fallen timber?

What has survived, though, are the hazel woods. They were the natural pioneer woodland here and their nuts must have been a valuable food source to the Stone Age settlers. They may even be advancing again as grazing animals drop off in numbers.

The Burren hazel woods come in all sizes. Some are so dense that you must crawl about them on your hands and knees. Others are growing in minimal soil or are grazed so hard back that you can experience, Gulliver-like, the bizarre sensation of wandering through a forest that comes up no higher than your chest. It is in these stunted woodlets on the barest rocks that you can also have the disorientating experience of seeing alpine flowers – gentian and mountain avens especially – growing under the trees.

I shoulder my way into one of the taller hazel groves, on the site of an Iron Age fort at Cathair Mhor. It is humid and hushed inside. The floor is strewn with boulders and fallen branches, and swathed in a blanket of moss up to eight inches thick in places. I creep about as softly as I can, but the moss still shows deep, accusing pits where my feet have been. For a moment I have a mad fancy that I may be the first person to have been in this particular corner of the wood since the Iron Age. It is, I suppose, more of a bower than a wood, and though it has primroses, blue-bells and orchids they are not growing in masses as in woods where the ground is more open, but in ones and twos wherever the moss is compact enough. And in the dappled shade at the edge of the woodlet I find my first specimen of the Irish spotted orchid – a pure white spike so distinctive to this part of the world that it has an Irish-Latin name – *Dactylorchis fuchsii* subsp. *okellyi* – after the Ballyvaughan nurseryman who discovered it.

The next day was what the Irish euphemistically call 'soft'. There was scudding low cloud and a threat of rain, and I decided to curb my puppyish scampering about the rocks and go on a more purposeful journey. I armed myself with T. D. Robinson's lyrical map of the Burren, which eschews contour lines in favour of outlines of the geological forms of terraces and cliffs (what he calls 'the grain of the land') and which is densely covered with the sites of cairns, ring forts, tombs and turloughs. It is a map – understandably, among these history-cheating rocks – organised around the sense of vision, not time.

In the hamlet of Turlough itself, just east of Ballyvaughan, I found a huge example of these mysterious pools, which during wet weather fill with water bubbling up through subterranean channels in the limestone, and drain the same way, sometimes in a matter of hours. This one was nearly half a mile across and maybe ten feet deep in places – only it was almost devoid of water. Cattle were grazing the flush of grass which follows flooding, and which makes the summer turloughs an important part of the Burren farming system.

I drove on south, and during a squall of rain stopped the car by a derelict farmhouse near Poulbaun. Up on the hills to the west I could see the slivers of stone, like crosses and hands, which have been jammed upright in the crags above the crumbling remains of ancient, curving enclosures. Even under louring skies they didn't seem like emblems of melancholy or hardship so much as, in Robinson's words, 'memorials to the tedium of the herdsman's life'.

A few miles on, just north of Kilnaboy, the relics of the triple cliff-fort, Cathair Chomain, circa AD 1000, looked scarcely more durable. The hazel woods were creeping up the hill towards it and the stone fortifications slowly collapsing into the scree. Just below it, precisely the same thing was happening to the shell of a lurid farm bungalow, built with blue and pink bricks circa 1958. And a few hundred yards further on, I saw the garden of a roadside cottage which, despite a shrine to Mary near the pergola, was being slowly reclaimed by the vast natural rockery outside.

Why has occupation been so casual and ephemeral here? What has repeatedly made people settle in numbers and then just walk away? There was famine, of course, during the nineteenth century, and a continual leakage of people ever since. But the visible remains of settlement in the Burren go back at least 3,000 years. There are sixty-six megalithic tombs dating from between 2000 and 1400 BC; nearly 500 ring forts (cathairs) and similar enclosures, from between 200 BC to the late medieval period; and many hundreds of farms, hovels and goat-huts abandoned since then.

I sat by one of the neolithic gallery graves at Creevagh and pondered this almost nomadic history. These communal tombs, made out of limestone rocks and topped with three giant slabs in the shape of a wedge, are the most enduring features of the landscape. Yet there is not the slightest air of gloom or Gothicness clinging to them. The tomb at Creevagh had wild flowers on its huge topping slab, and turf that may have been there since it was first raised. Inside the wedge it looked friendly enough to sleep in. I wondered if animals ever bedded down there in bad weather, as the last Irish bears had in Ailwee cave, near Ballyvaughan. The early human settlers were apparently more claustrophobic: no evidence of human residence has been found in any of the local caves. Even then this ringing landscape seemed to be saying the same thing to its visitors: stay on top, hang loose, move on.

A freewheeling spirit certainly infuses the few settlements that have survived in the Burren. I spent my last day, a Saturday, meandering round them – and rapidly wished I'd been based in one, instead of out in the backlands. In Kilfenora, there is a Burren visitors' centre, owned and run by the people of the village and showing videos and displays of the region's history and ecology. Doolin, away on the west coast above the Cliffs of Moher, is a small but rumbustious village, a centre of local craftspeople and of Irish music. O'Connor's bar was a furious place at lunchtime, full of old hippies, fishermen, travellers of the more adventurous sort, and ad hoc musicians. I supped a stew and watched the place start jigging to a solo penny-whistler who just happened to start up between pints. Musical tastes here are very eclectic: the Dutchman pounding his glass of Guinness on the table next to mine was wearing a Pogues T-shirt; and in Lisdoonvarna, the live music that was advertised in every bar on every day of the week ranged from show band and country and western to unaccompanied Celtic ballads.

Lisdoonvarna is the eccentric capital of the Burren, and the place to take its human pulse. It is a spa town, a place of festivals and reunions. On the walls of the bars there are countless pictures of one-time regulars, news clippings about emigrants, mottoes and snippets of cracker-barrel philosophy. In the autumn, after harvest, there is a celebrated 'matchmaking week' here, when bachelor farmers of a certain age come in the hope of finding wives. In 1990 they rounded the season off by holding the World Barbecue Championship here. Any moment you expect the travelling medicine show to ride into town.

I remembered the opening words of the Kilfenora Centre's introductory video about the Burren: 'Here on the farthest western edge of the Old World . . .' and realised that the whole region feels at times like frontier country. But it is no badlands, and deserves (and is usually given) deep respect.

Down in the extreme south-east of the Burren is Mullaghmore, one of the most hauntingly beautiful places in Europe. It is dominated by a dramatically buckled limestone hill, whose bowed layers of rock glow soft pink and grey behind a pure blue lough. You can walk for hours in its foothills, through drifts of orchids and thickets of yellow-flowered shrubby cinquefoil, crossing streams and fingers of water on natural stepping stones scratched by otters, and smelling the warm honey and cream of the burnet roses. The whole enchanted scene is visible five miles away. It is Ireland's Ayers Rock, as close to being a sacred place as is possible in the sceptical West.

Yet as I write it is threatened by a development scheme of scarcely credible barbarousness. It is here (rather than in one of the already developed villages) that the Irish Office of Public Works have decided to deposit a new Interpretation Centre, along with thirty acres of car park, roads and 'landscaped walkways'. One can only hope that if the project comes to fruition it will be subject to the same trial by rock as every other human claim staked out in this exuberant, flirtatious landscape.

1991

Winter in the Camargue

It is only from the air that you can get a notion of just how thoroughly the Camargue is awash with water. For more than sixty miles along the Mediterranean seaboard, west of Marseilles, the Rhône delta frays into a fantastic labyrinth of marsh-fringed creeks and lagoons.

The landing approach to Montpellier airport is low over this seaward edge, and from this angle the fingers of land seemed to be existing purely on sufferance. The autoroutes looked like lost causeways and Montpellier's runways about as secure as sinking aircraft carriers.

Then, just as we banked for landing, I glimpsed a scene that seemed to sum up the two faces of the Camargue. Between the sea and the lagoons were the jutting, pyramidal blocks of the new holiday complex at La Grande Motte, and, paddling in the choppy water in front of them, a hundred or so of the Camargue's most ancient and celebrated citizens, the flamingos, glowing pale pink in the setting sun.

I had been looking for flamingos when I was last here. It was high summer in the early 1960s, before the French government hatched their scheme for the development of the Languedoc coast, and before La Grande Motte's architect had bragged that 'to start the resort a hard core was necessary to mark the countryside with its virile presence'. The Camargue then had seemed virile enough already. There were riotous bands of gypsies, black bulls raging through the streets in the non-lethal *course à la cocarde*, and the *gardians*, the Camargue cowboys, high-stepping through the marshes on their white horses. It was a hectic and colourful prospect, and I was glad I had hired a cine camera for the trip. It was unbeatable as a virile shoulder accessory, but I did have one serious filmic ambition: to picture flamingos wading amongst the samphire in what I couldn't help seeing as an exotic version of East Anglia.

So, one morning before it got too hot, kitted out with bottles of grape juice and feeling like real explorers, we slunk, then crawled, across the blinding white salt pans where the flamingos summered. We got within about 300 yards of a huge flock before they tired of our graceless progress and took to the air – an immense, billowing surf of salmon and scarlet. I pressed the Bolex shutter until the film ran out.

Nature had rather more than the last laugh on this occasion. A few days later the camera was swamped by a monstrous wave as I was flaunting it at some starlets on a Riviera beach, all but ruining the mechanism and exhausting my holiday budget. As for the flamingo footage, when I projected it back at home, the distant birds were indistinguishable from the dust specks on the lens.

In winter, I reckoned, things would be different – especially twenty-odd years on. Unlike a good number of exotic Mediterranean birds, many of the flamingos stayed on over the cold months, and I rather fancied seeing such fabulous creatures in landscape stripped of all the machismo and forced picturesqueness of summer. But it proved hard to prise the Camargue entirely free of its theatrical aura. My two companions made wildlife documentaries, for a start. There was a Franco-American film crew staying at our hotel in Arles, here, mystifyingly, to make an episode for the TV series *William Tell*. Even the hotel manager had a winningly histrionic approach to his job. One morning at breakfast, he played out a tense one-acter about the time he was caught out in the street as the Allies were bombing the town's bridge across the Rhône in 1944. He has a photo taken from one of the bombers hanging ambiguously on his wall.

Arles straddles the Rhône, and is almost at the apex of 180,000 acres of marshland that have formed in its delta. It is, in consequence, on a major bird migration route. But it still surprised us that the first bird we saw on our first morning was a peregrine falcon, jinking amongst the muddled roofscape of the town centre and causing consternation amongst its morose pigeons. It was only when we drove out of the shelter of the town that we realised the hapless falcon had been blown clean down the Rhône. The mistral had arrived, the cold wind that funnels down the river valley from the mountains, and which can blow for days on end.

As we drove south in the comfort of the car, it actually proved welcome, and lent a bit of briskness to the landscape. Much of the northern reaches of the Camargue has been drained, desalinated and irrigated, and given over to rice growing. It is flat and monotonous, but neither this nor the wind seemed to be the slightest deterrent to the birds. Buzzards floated over the rice stubble. Marsh harriers hawked along the thickets of tamarisk and giant reed that fringe the irrigation channels. And wherever there were bigger patches of reed and open water, there was always the chance of a little egret, its long, dazzling white plumage in disarray in the gale.

Further south were more traditional Camargue prospects of marshy pastures, with bulls and white horses and the first saline pools. The lagoons were covered with immense rafts of duck. A small group of flamingos huddled together against the wind, into which they projected four feet above the ducks.

Beating against it ourselves, we sympathised with them. This particular mistral did not seem to be especially cold or powerful (though they have been known to stop trains in their tracks). But it did have a persistent, nagging bitterness that eventually made us feel raddled and tetchy. It could have been a lot worse: it was during a December mistral that Van Gogh, Arles' most famous inhabitant, cut off his ear.

Later in the afternoon the wind dropped a little, and we meandered further south, down amongst the salt settling pans, where brackish water is left to evaporate until the salt can be scraped away. Salt is the Camargue's major industry, and more than a million tons are produced every year. The pans make a bizarre landscape, too briny to support many birds in winter, but with an odd crystalline life of their own. The wind was whipping the salt liquor into foam along the edges of the pans, where it hung like unset meringue, glinting erratically in the low sun.

Even though it was early December, the air seemed to have a lustrous Mediterranean glow, and I think it must have gone to our heads. We set off to drive back to Arles, but kept finding the sun swinging hypnotically to our right hand. Every so often, as if part of a conspiracy, hand-painted notice boards advertising 'Marc et Mireille's café du poissons' appeared, always pointing enticingly to the left. We were among the natural lagoons now, on tracks that sometimes seemed to be below the level of the water. Soon we were driving on the precarious sandy edges of the lagoons themselves, and the germ of an island-dweller's ancestral dread began to surface, not to be calmed by the knowledge that the Mediterranean isn't tidal.

We reached Marc et Mireille's in the end. It was a converted caravan propped up on a beach. We were hopelessly lost, and put our predicament – and our maps – before a group of wind surfers camped out on the beach. They were vastly amused, but showed us the way back – and also several ways that would *not* get us out.

Our unintended diversion proved a happy accident in the end, because it gave us the best views of flamingos of our whole stay. There was a large flock in a lagoon close to the shore, not much more than fifty yards from the bank. As we moved closer, though, they edged further away. I suppose they were simply wading, in their slow-motion, fastidious way. But they looked for all the world as if they were *gliding* over the water, like a fleet of dhows, or the swimmers in an elaborate Esther Williams routine.

Flamingos have such an extraordinary appearance that it is hard to see them as birds whilst they are grounded. But once they are in the air – in tight formations of startling black and red wings, with their long deep-red legs held stiffly back to serve as tailplanes – they are breathtaking.

Each morning we would wake to a cloudless sky and walk up to the nearest square to see if the tops of the plane trees were still shaking in the wind. They usually were, but the mistral didn't restrict us that much. We visited the vast Étang de Vaccarès, the heart of the National Reserve, where most of the flamingos breed. At dusk we parked the car by the side of a road and watched more than fifty marsh harriers come swooping and toying in the wind as they returned to their communal roost in the surrounding reedbeds. We spent a few hours in the stony wastes of Le Crau, on the eastern edge of the marshes, but it was a Sunday, and the hunters were out in force. We made a brief visit to the ruined village of Les Baux, in the limestone hills known as Les Alpilles, north of the region, and would have explored it more, but that afternoon the mistral was at its fiercest. It sucked our map (marked up with various choice bird sites) right out of the car, and whisked it off in the direction of the artillery on Le Crau. We ended up cowering in the car park of what is reputedly one of the best restaurants in France, watching black redstarts and wall creepers and a blue rock thrush with plumage the texture of shot silk darting about the limestone crags.

The day before we were due to leave the mistral blew itself out, and we decided to go back to Les Alpilles, where there was a chance of seeing an eagle owl. The hills are only a few miles from Arles, and their low, jagged peaks form the background to Van Gogh's painting of a blue cart. On the way we passed the *William Tell* film crew rigging up lights on the roof of the Abbey of Montmajour, ready for a night shoot.

Our destination was a track at the foot of the hills. On one side were a few small olive groves; on the other, stretches of aromatic Mediterranean scrub, sweeping up to two limestone crags with a wooded pass between them. We got out of the car and waited. It was an almost perfect evening, still and not too cold. A thin moon appeared over the peaks, and as the sky darkened over the tracts of evergreen oak and flowering rosemary it was hard to believe it was winter.

At about five-thirty, the eagle owl called, a deep, croaking hoot, sounding as if it was uttered at the bottom of a barrel. I missed its first flight between the two crags, but picked it up perched on top of a cliff, presumably watching us. Through the binoculars it looked like a dead log, standing on end. When it finally launched itself into the air, it was as if an immense gargoyle had broken free of the cliff. It sailed out against the now purple sky for nearly twenty seconds without flapping its wings, and vanished in the general direction of the Abbey of Montmajour. Eagle owls have a wing span of five feet and appetites to match. They have been known to eat dogs, sheep and small eagles, and I would not put a young lighting engineer past them. The French, with an untypical show of respect for a bird, call it 'le grand-duc'.

On our final day I looked in on the Musée Arletan. It was rather like an extended attic, with a series of rooms stuffed with furniture, folk-costumes, bulls' heads, herbalists' potions, and even a fully mocked-up interior of a *gardian*'s cabin. The first floor was more organised, however, and unfolded the fascinating economic and cultural history of the Camargue. There were displays on the use of reed and willow, on local boat- and house-building techniques, on the salt industry (with some exquisite salt-crusted curios made by dipping toys and models repeatedly in the salt pans), and a fearsome exhibit on bird-trapping, which showed a nineteenth-century marshman swatting small migrants with something resembling an enormous cricket bat.

What the museum demonstrated was that the Camargue has not been a true wilderness for a very long time. It has been intimately (but respectfully) exploited for at least 2,000 years, and its wildlife has coexisted with this use, helped by the alchemy that occurs when sunshine and water mix. But these are difficult times for the marshes. Small-scale farming and pasturing are in retreat here as everywhere, and tourism and development are growing in intensity. The saving grace for the Camargue may be that at last the French are beginning to become concerned about the conservation of their own wildlife and landscapes. Flying back over a Massif Central blanketed by snow I remembered the extraordinary story we had been told about the flamingo rescue operation mounted during the terrible freeze-up of January 1985. About half the region's 20,000 flamingos remained in France during the cold spell, and of these nearly 3,000 died. Another 1,000 were found close to starvation. These were wrapped in blankets and taken off to be looked after in homes and schools along the Camargue coast. They were fed on rice and dog food; and a further twenty tons of rice (equivalent to the annual consumption of a small town) was put down for the birds still sticking it out in the wild.

When the freeze-up ended, the birds were released. Not one of them had died, and the people of the Camargue had shown their affection for the real bird behind the tourist symbol.

1988

The Lubéron

The Montagne du Lubéron, a flower-decked limestone bastion fifteen miles north of Aix-en-Provence, has been a favourite retreat of the French middle classes since the last century. Full of stone-built hillside villages and poised between the airy woods of the Massif and the warm south, it is a kind of Mediterranean Cotswolds, picturesque and pastoral but rapidly losing its indigenous inhabitants. In 1977 the government designated the whole region as a Parc Régional Naturel, in the hope of reviving its rural communities and achieving a *modus vivendi* between tourism and the traditional economy. Since then the Parc has become a showpiece for changing French attitudes towards conservation. It has a reputation for magnificent wild flowers and *aspects naturels* and seemed a place worth chancing an early spring visit.

We were based at an elegantly converted farmhouse in Les Baux, a medieval fortress town and one-time troglodytes' colony, perched on a sheer spur of rock at the western end of the limestone ridge. From the hotel garden we could just make out what would be our terrain for the next few days, a pale swell of hills looking worryingly distant and austere.

But our hotel was too comfortable to make us bothered about the daily haul into the Parc. And the town itself is a salutary reminder of the cavalier way that history and climate can treat settlements in wild countryside.

In medieval times Les Baux was best known as a centre of the troubadour tradition. But it was also a stronghold of troublesome Protestant warlords, and in 1632 Cardinal Richelieu ordered its castle and ramparts to be destroyed. When the surrounding marshlands were subsequently drained and cultivated most of the remaining population moved down onto the plain. Les Baux became little more than a ghost town. When we arrived it was under siege by mistral-driven rainstorms, and busloads of French schoolchildren were doing passable imitations of troglodytes sheltering in the decaying archways and rock-gouged dwelling spaces.

Next day the mistral was still gusting, and the billboards trumpeting 'La Route du Soleil' along the road from Les Baux to the Lubéron looked absurdly optimistic. In summer, though, it is clearly a different story. There were forest conservation posters, too, beside the roads, nailed up above blackened pine stumps and ground seared down to the bare rock, evidence of what an inflammable brew sun and holidaymakers can be. 'Pensez à la fôret' and 'La fôret embellit la vie' they read, an indication, perhaps, that two summers of rampant forest fires were having the same effect on French tree-consciousness as two hurricanes have had on ours.

But the climate has also made the southern foothills of the Lubéron perfect for fruit-growing. To the south of the hills the Durance valley is full of orchards of cherries, pears and peaches, trained and pruned in every conceivable way. There were cordons, espaliers, *double* espaliers. In the village squares even the plane trees were pleached.

We left the valley near Merindol and climbed up towards the ridge, through tiers of pine-sheltered holiday villas. Then they thinned out, and we were in the *garigue*, the tangle of aromatic shrubs and herbs that covers much of the hill country of the Mediterranean. On cue the sun came out and, as if a wand had been waved over them, clouds of butterflies wafted into the air – swallowtails, clouded yellows, adonis blues. Buzzards and black kites materialised in the thermals, and we found early spider orchids lurking amongst the juniper and thyme. After our some-what gloomy first glimpses from the hotel, the Lubéron began to look like the natural paradise it was reputed to be. But these high plateaux seemed to have been virtually abandoned by agriculture. The surviving farmhouses have been expensively converted, and livid patches of swimming-pool blue shimmered incongruously in a landscape of withering vines and burgeoning Mediterranean scrub.

Further on, the wildwood was making even more impressive advances. Stretching along the Lubéron's western ridge is a cedar forest, which the Parc authorities are taking steps to protect. The day we were there the through-road had been closed specifically for the benefit of the wildlife and vegetation. This was carefully and courteously explained on notice boards, along with the story of the cedar trees. Although they are no longer native to Provence, they had apparently grown here 20,000 years ago. These new speci-mens had arrived here ('*par eaux*', the board said mysteriously) from the Atlas Mountains in Morocco in the 1860s. Presumably they were planted, but they are already sizeable enough to be setting their own seedlings and nourishing a host of fungi. Visitors were welcome to pick these, the notices advised, provided it was done '*avec mesure*'.

On the damper north-facing slopes, the cedar forest merges with homely oakwoods. To the south it dissolves in a haze of rosemary, box and cistus scrub studded with grape-hyacinths and jonquils. Much of the current vegetation of Provence is the result of the deforestation and over-exploitation of poor soils. So the return of woodland cover is generally welcomed, especially now that cultivation itself is retreating even further down the hill. The old crops of silkworms and lavender and even olives have largely vanished. So have the communities that grew them. The hilltop villages look dramatically beautiful clinging to the steep limestone terraces, but have the feel of open-air museums.

Bonnieux, where the medieval ramparts still survive, is full of art galleries and up-market estate agents. Menerbes, ten kilometres to the west, is an eyrie of a village, and once a strategic fortress during the conflicts between Catholics and Protestants that raged violently in the Lubéron in the sixteenth century. The most stunning of the villages is Roussillon, which stands on a rare outcrop of red sandstone. The buildings are almost entirely constructed out of this local rock, which comes in something like twenty different shades of ochre and gives the village the sense of being a piece of rare confectionary. But there was no one in the restaurants, and the tourists in the streets walked in slow, reverential motion.

We found a more cheerful refuge in Lacoste and sat outside a hillside bar, eating omelettes a foot long and watching the returning swallows coasting up the valley. The village, where the Marquis de Sade had his estate in the late eighteenth century, had a distinctly bohemian feel and there was a boisterous group of expatriate English artists and teachers at the bar. With them was a prime specimen of an increasingly common species in the wilder areas of rural Europe: the off-the-tracks know-all showing off his collection of culture bites as lesser mortals display their car stickers.

He would, I suspect, have felt completely at home in the august museum of *bories* at Gordes. The *bories*, a feature of local vernacular architecture, are shelters built – usually in the rough shape of igloos – from layered limestone slabs, much as dry-stone walls are constructed. They were normally used as sheep-pens or barns, but the earliest date from the Iron Age and probably served as dwelling places. In accordance with upwardly mobile Lubéron trends, a group of the best have been spruced up, gentrified and preserved in an outdoor museum. We got a more vivid sense of them by prowling around the patchwork of orchid-strewn scrub and pastures near the villages, where many still have a working role as outhouses.

On our penultimate day it was perceptibly warmer, and we opted to explore a south-west-facing hillside that looked – from the map at least – as if it might squeeze the most from the thin sunshine.

It was better than we could ever have imagined. Just a few yards from where we parked, the *garigue* was thick with tiny jonquils, rock-roses and budding wild pinks. A few hundred yards further up the narrow hill road, the irises began. They were *Iris chamaeiris*, very short-stemmed but with big blowsy blossoms, in a huge variety of mauves and blues. Some, coloured with striations of deep Tyrian purple, had a bouquet like that of Florentine irises. There was another extraordinary scent experience a little higher up. Amid sheets of stubby, dark-blue grape hyacinths and pink valerian, so thick that in places they obscured the powdery white rock below, were spikes of the buttercup *Ranunculus gramineus*, with the clear, penetrating scent of jasmine. And at the top, up to our knees in wild thyme and looking out across billows of snowy mespilus on the crags, we realised that we were standing amongst clumps of star-flowered yellow tulips, arranged as exquisitely about the limestone terraces as if they had been in a rock-garden. I doubt that we had covered much more than a mile through the scrub, yet had strolled amongst galleries and bowers of flowers the like of which I have seen nowhere else.

We had a celebratory feast that evening, on the kind of *haut paysan* cuisine in which our hotel specialised: tangy aperitifs distilled from local herbs and flowers, a lasagne made with langoustines, home-made brawn, *lotte* and rice from the Camargue (only ten miles to the south), rabbit, and sheep and goat cheeses.

When we got up the next morning, departure day, we found the weather had leaped straight into summer. Alpine swift packs were hurtling round the fortifications of Les Baux against a clear blue sky, and nightingales and hoopoes were singing in the valley. It was Mediterranean weather, tourist weather, but maybe not the weather for that wild alpine garden on the Lubéron slopes that we had probably seen on its best day of the season.

1990

Crete

The coastline of northern Crete is an embarrassing reminder of the fickle power of tourism. It is lined with rows of unfinished apartment blocks, identically framed in reinforced concrete, and already beginning to look like prefabricated antiquities. They were begun in a hopeful rush during Crete's tourist boom, and put on hold, maybe permanently, when the fashionable destinations moved further east. They are just the latest in a long line of blights caused by culture contact. It is no consolation recalling that the Cretans were probably the first overseas visitors to the British Isles, and that we are, as it were, just returning the compliment. When the Minoans sailed into the newly opened English Channel nearly 6,000 years ago, they set the mould for evolution of the English landscape. It's them we have to thank for pastoral farming, the downs on the southern chalk-hills, the first long-distance trackways, and perhaps for that persistent thread of nature-worship in our own culture. Summer-season discos and a ravaged coastline seem a poor swap.

But flying out in the middle of April for the spring flowers and migrating birds, our little party had banished guilt under a sense of missionary purpose. We were, the brochures had assured us, amongst the pioneers of a new approach to tourism, which could turn it from a ruiner of landscapes into an economically powerful force for conservation.

The Cretan version of this idea had come from the Norfolk Naturalists Trust. Anne Cryer, who had been in thrall to the island since she first visited as a student, had begun to organise wildlife holidays for Trust members in 1986. The island has long been famous as a botanical paradise, a stronghold of wild bulbous species and hundreds of indigenous rarities. But Anne had also discovered another treasure – a string of lagoons on the north coast at Gouves, sixteen kilometres east of Heraklion. For an arid island, perched on one of the trans-Mediterranean migration routes, these amounted to an oasis. Even on those early visits it became obvious that the lagoons had an exceptional tally of migrant birds. Flocks of three different species of heron called in, as did flamingos, black-winged stilts and the piratical Eleonora's falcon, which haunts the seaways round the Mediterranean islands, picking off swallows and martins. In all, 168 species had been logged by 1989. Alas, there was one serious problem. Greece hadn't yet caught up with Europe's environmental awakening, and the lagoons, which are owned by the villagers of Gouves, were being used as a communal rubbish pit.

Anne returned to Crete with a plan to save the lagoons by promoting them as one of the key attractions of the area, dangling the carrot of planeloads of green tourists. By a stroke of luck the lagoons lie right next to a commodious hotel, and there was no difficulty in getting the cooperation of the manager, who also happened to be a local politician. Things went well to begin with. The rubbish dumping was stopped, and the hotel agreed to a hide being built at the edge of its garden, overlooking the lagoons. The prospect of watching stilts within hailing distance of the poolside bar seemed a considerable bonus point for the jaunt.

The hide was clearly visible as the coach rolled up to the dazzling frontage – more Polynesian than Aegean – of the hotel. But the lagoons, strewn with hard core and not helped by the drought which had set in weeks earlier than usual, looked rather miserable. So did Anne. She had been biting her lip during the journey, and confessed that there had been some new developments. The Greek elections were only a few weeks away, and local political pressure had made the informal agreement over dumping go by the board. Nearly a third of the pools had been filled in. And now the villagers were putting phase two of their own development scheme into operation, and building a football pitch over the top.

Outside the hotel there were forbidding rows of coaches from Wuppertal and Dortmund. Inside, the open-plan lobby was full of brisk track-suited couples and posters announcing tennis knock-outs and cycling races. The slightest flickers of disdain could be glimpsed on the British faces. It looked as if the scene were set for an old-style Athenian tournament, or maybe an eisteddfod, with several ancient European tribes displaying their ways of celebrating the land.

I was glad this hotel had been finished. My room had an extra-ordinary view, over the garden and swimming pool to the sea, which was no more than fifty metres away. When I drew back the shutters at about 6 a.m. the first round (Ritual Improvisation in Small Groups) was already under way. Out in the pool virile Wuppertalians in black wet suits were toiling through the water, pausing only for little bursts of aerobics on the side. Below my balcony a dozen or so Brits straggled back from the daily stroll to catch the dawn migrants, telescopes over their shoulders like retreating guerrillas. 'Anything about?' 'Not a lot. Eleonoras in from the sea. Flock of purple herons down on the lagoons.' A *flock* of purple herons! All I could manage were four night herons that had clattered out of the willows next to my balcony, where they'd presumably been roosting. Down in the garden Sardinian warblers darted amongst the lawn-sprayers as non-chalantly as robins. Round one to the birds, I reckoned, for economy of performance.

Over breakfast I asked Doug Ireland, our West Country guide, about the herons, trying to disguise my chagrin at having missed them. There had been more than fifty, migrating north before the sun got up, and he reckoned they'd been disorientated by the low mist over the mountains. 'You have to get up early to see these things,' said Doug, in his off-duty sergeant's voice that we came to know and love.

I never did get my metabolism in a condition to cope with the dawn patrol, and had to endure these humiliating tallies every morning. But that first day the whole party – about thirty strong – had an introductory tour of what was left of the lagoons in the company of Doug, Ivan Loades, our botanist, and Chris Gibson, who worked for the Nature Conservancy Council and passed most of his holidays as a guide. There were still plenty of birds about. By the side of the river that fed the lagoon, tufts of giant reed and tamarisk rang with the croaks of great reed warblers ('You'll believe a frog can fly,' someone quipped) and the whiplash calls of Cetti's warblers. A little egret got up from the river, and wafted away like a windblown shawl. By midday the temperature was already approaching eighty degrees, and Chris Gibson spotted some terrapins basking on the muddy edges of the river, their shells tilted up to catch the sun.

But it was the plants that were most extraordinary. Down on the beach, amongst debris blowing in from the rubbish-filled lagoons, were legions of wiry creepers and spreaders: a beautiful bi-coloured sea-lavender, naturalised mesembryanthemums from southern Africa, and the first of Crete's endemic species (there are 140-plus, almost a tenth of the entire flora), a dwarf chamomile with yellow button flowers.

As we moved further up the beach into the scrub zone, the varieties of armour against heat and drought and browsing animals multiplied. There were waxy-leaved sea-hollies and a wild cucumber with exploding pods that sprayed would-be predators with a mixture of seeds and toxic juice. There was a shrubby burnet covered with a protective net of what looked exactly like chicken wire. Mostly, though, the plants were spiny. The thyme was spiny. The saltwort was spiny. Even the local species of wild asparagus was spiny, and had an alarming resemblance to strands from a flagellant's whip.

That afternoon we walked onto the lower reaches of the steep rocky hill that rose behind the village. Everyone called this 'the

Mickey Mouse ears', after the landmark on the top – two huge saucer-shaped US listening devices, pointed unambiguously at Libya. They were a favourite loafing site for griffon vultures, and several times we saw one of these feathered planks – six foot in wing span – soar out into the thermals. They are the most languid of birds, and when they have gorged themselves at a carcass they simply tip themselves off a rock ledge. I don't think I have ever seen one so much as flap a wing.

We were amongst olive groves here, and in a different kind of landscape. This was the maquis, the low scrub that covers much of the island. It is full of shrubs familiar in their garden versions – brooms, euphorbias, rue, lavender, myrtle – many of them aromatic from the oily coating that helps their leaves conserve moisture. But the strangest plant was the dragon arum, a relative of our cuckoo-pint whose 'flower' is a vast purple hood up to three feet long, sheathing a chocolate-brown spadix that smells of rotten meat. It grows quite promiscuously on roadsides, amongst the olives, at the edge of farmyards, sometimes out of cracks in the rock. Edward Lear, who travelled through the island in the spring of 1864, saw masses of the plant on the same mid-April date. He described it in his journals as 'brutal-filthy yet picturesque', which seemed a fair summing-up.

But the island as a whole he found far from picturesque. It was too rugged for his formal Claudian tastes, too much a place of muddled foreground detail, and he complained constantly about the lack of the kind of 'drawable' scenes he had found in earlier travels in Italy and the Near East. He loved the birds, however, and his sightings for that day – orioles, hoopoes, bee-eaters – would have made him a star at the ritual into which we were initiated in the evening. After dinner, as the fashion-shows and talent contests reached clamorous heights round the bar, our contingent retired to a side room for the Calling of the Birds. The rules were simple but strict. Doug Ireland would intone the family names of Crete's 300-plus species, and members of the party would give details of their sightings that day. Precision was the thing. Our gleeful report of the languorous vultures, and the peregrine falcon that had streaked above us while we were rummaging in the maquis, was greeted with the phrase *'How many?'* – uttered in the tones of a man whose patience with the vagueness of his fellows was frequently tested, but inexhaustible.

The party – a mix largely of teachers, librarians, health workers, local government officers – were well able to hold their own in this kind of banter. It was the loosest possible kind of holiday, and over the next few days people could join in the organised activities as and when they wished. There were trips to Knossos, to the salt pans round the peninsula of Spinalonga, and down to the estuary at Agia Triada. Botanically, though, it was not proving a good year, and the drought and unseasonably high temperatures meant that most of the spring flowers had already been shrivelled up – at least on low-lying sites.

So with a friend I decided to take a private trip due south, over the hill country in the centre of the island and down to the coast. Away from the arid and over-developed coastal strip things looked decidedly brighter. The scrub got thicker and richer the further we drove inland, with dazzling shows of cistus and phlomis. The masses of exquisite white bells on the styrax bushes looked almost oriental amongst all this colour. Then, on the foothills, there were cyclamen and orchids scattered in the dappled shade of the ever-green oaks – including the delectable *Orchis papilionacea*, whose name exactly catches the flower's look of a cluster of folded purple butterflies. We found more Cretan endemics too: a woody goosegrass, whose sticky tendrils emerged from a solid trunk, like a cat-o'-nine-tails, and the island's most celebrated native, Cretan ebony. This member of the pea family with deep pink flowers and silver-haired leaves grows in great clusters on the steep roadsides and white limestone cliffs, and from a distance has the look of a mass of heather lightly dusted with hoarfrost.

We ate grilled chicken under an immense pollarded plane in Ano Viannos, and, along with what seemed the entire village, watched the day's drama – a miniature bulldozer trying to create some kind of viaduct under the street. Pollarding was another sustainable technique probably developed by the Minoans, and it was surprising and depressing to find how little forest cover remained when we journeyed further south in the afternoon. As we began to tip downhill towards the coast, the landscape grew as brown and barren as north Africa. After an hour of hairpin bends on a worsening dirt track with nothing visible in front of us except miles of bare mountains, the first tremors of panic began at the possibility that we might have somehow left the road system altogether. The pot-holes became bigger and the space between track and cliff narrower. Then, quite sickeningly, we were motoring along what seemed to be a ridge, with sheer drops on both sides. The mountain had simply been dynamited apart. We'd strayed into an agrobusiness version of terrace cultivation, not for grapes or maize, but for what we could now see spreading out below us – a vast honeycombed metropolis of polythene greenhouses. Not a soul was about but through rips in the brown plastic we could see that the houses were stuffed with two of Crete's principal exports – carnations and bananas. Like most cash crops, they didn't seem to have benefited the locals much. When we finally arrived at a village it was like something from a Steinbeck novel – a sad collection of shacks and run-down bars, with piece-workers leaning listlessly against the walls.

Crete's landscape and economy have been buffeted by centuries of occupation and over-grazing, and now have to endure the mixed blessings of the Common Agricultural Policy. But the barrenness of the south and the whole coastal belt has just as much to do with their intense heat and summer drought (the Libyan Desert is only 400 miles to the south). To see how lush Crete can still be you must travel to the west of the island. The hills south of Rethymnon have something of the look of the Lake District. There are woods of plane and the native, spreading cypress in the ravines, and meadows of orchids and turban buttercups.

This is also gorge country. There are more than a hundred gorges in the island, mostly ranging north–south and ending up at the sea. Driving down one afternoon to Plakias (where there is a small colony of the island's strangest endemic, the stumpy and wistful Cretan palm) we passed through the gorge of Kotsiphou. It is only a little wider than the road at its northern end, and alpine swifts and crag martins flickered about the cliff faces high above. Further south the gorge widened out, and we stopped to watch the birds of prey gliding in the thermals. There were kestrels, buzzards, a brief glimpse of a peregrine, and two gorgeous golden eagles, soaring at such an obliging angle to the sun that I could see the pale patches on their rumps and wings.

Then, watching a group of griffons idling above the furthest ridge, I saw a different bird join the circle. It had the jizz of an immense falcon more than a vulture, with narrow scimitar wings and an extraordinary diamond-shaped tail. I was sure, though I had never seen one before, that it was Crete's supreme bird, and Europe's largest and rarest vulture, the fabled lammergeier. Lammergeiers haunt the most remote mountainous reaches, and have the unique habit of dropping bones from a height onto rocks to split them open for the marrow. Watching this one circling with its cousins, a dark, ominous crossbow, outstretched wings held dead level, it seemed like an archaeopteryx, something half-remembered from another age. I remembered John Fowles' account of resting while mountain climbing not far from here, and suddenly finding a lammergeier hanging twenty feet above his head, 'its great wings feathering and flexed to the wind current, a savage hooked beak tilted down towards me. I lay as still as a stone, like Sinbad under the rock. For some ten seconds the great bird and I were transfixed, in a kind of silent dialogue.' I wondered what kind of reception my more distant encounter would get from the House Meeting that evening.

It got, needless to say, a steely inquisition from Doug Ireland. Lammergeiers were one of the most longed-for species, and ever since one had been spotted, stuffed and mounted over the bar in a mountain taverna, sightings had been greeted with scepticism. I still do not know if my record was accepted. But after nearly a week everyone was willing to have a go at bird-log banter, sure enough of their own skills – and Doug's – to risk spoof sightings and irreverent quips.

'Any shearwaters?'

'Cory's. Lots of them. Over the sea.'

'*How many*, Janet?'

Janet, the librarian, who had been gently ribbed all week for her disorganised vagueness over the red-throated pipit populations, replied quick as a flash, 'Two thousand five hundred, if I heard you correctly this morning.' Peter the planning officer, a master of one-liners, logged a swan he had spotted in the Knossos murals. 'Almost certainly mute.' Richard, who had made something of a cabaret act out of his sightings of sparrows, received huge applause for rising to the new challenge of greenfinches. 'How many?' '*Four*. Outside the taverna. *Before* lunch.'

In the bar, Wuppertal was demolishing the small Dutch contingent in a ballroom-dancing competition. I wondered if our evening routine, a cross between Bingo and ornithological Mastermind, was just a more decorous British version of holiday sports. Or worse, a kind of ecological colonialism. I can only hope that it was making some small contribution to the logging of the biological resources of what is still only a patchily known island.

On our last day we went out to the plain of Lassithi, and had a depressing view of the direction Cretan land-use is currently taking. Lassithi is a high plateau, perhaps the dried-out remains of a prehistoric lake, and is an oasis of rich soil amongst the mountains. We were due to walk straight across, a comparatively easy tramp of about seven kilometres on the flat. But it was blazing hot, the wind was blowing up sandstorms, no one was quite sure of the right path, and we ended up straggling for hours amongst the parched fields. All over the plain were the remains of hundreds of small windmills, once used for irrigation. Now the water is pumped electrically. But the soil was still desperately dry, and the crops looked in a dejected state. Tractors and mules passed each other, harrowing adjacent strips. Cretan men, lounging under trees, urged their wives on to greater efforts with the hoes, and seemed unsurprised by the sight of this gaggle of mad English people hiking across the prairie in the afternoon sun.

A scarce swallowtail butterfly took a shine to one of our number's blue anorak, and we heard a quail giving its persistent, knife-whetting call out in the fields. But there was precious little natural life about and a stench of pesticide in the air. We thought we glimpsed a man broadcasting seed, but he was strewing fertiliser pellets, by hand. It was an image which seemed to sum up this place, caught – as Crete itself is, in a way – between two different attitudes towards nature and the land.

1989

PART THREE

Land-Art

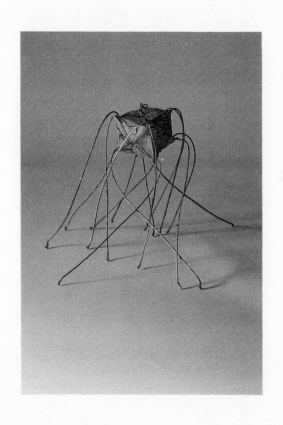

Patrick Wright and the Heritage Question

Is 'heritage' a bit like the lustre on a fish's scales, fading the moment the hapless specimen is caught, preserved, stuffed in a glass case? Does the exterior appearance of a landscape reflect its inner life, or just the fantasies of its observers? Patrick Wright has already shown himself a trenchant commentator on these questions in *On Living in an Old Country: The National Past in Contemporary Britain* (1985). His new book [*A Journey Through Ruins: The Last Days of London*, 1991] carries the argument into the intimate and feisty territory of his own quarter of London's East End, and is composed with all the magpie curiosity of a landscape artist. Wright picks through the bric-a-brac of Hackney like a concrete sculptor, teasing meanings out of vandalised phone boxes, council street maps, a copy of the *Market Rasen Mail* which he picks up from a West Indian newsagent on Dalston Lane. He is a sympathetic recorder, too, of the human communities which trade in these messages and artefacts, and especially of their tribulations during the break-up of what he calls 'the post-war consensus', when ideas such as a common future and the public good could still be talked about without embarrassment, and even Prime Ministers believed there was such a thing as society.

Wright is a materialist in the best sense of the word, and it is *objects*, notionally solid but hugely volatile in the cauldron of the inner city, that are the landmarks of his book. He sketches mordant portraits of the alienated and 'atomised' spaces of the notorious tower blocks on the Holly Street Estate, and trails the disassembled treasures of English Big Houses (urban and rural) as they lose one set of privileged meanings here only to gain another as instant period decor 'on Wall Street's fiftieth floor'. Even Hackney's drinking water becomes a metaphorical common stream: agitated by compulsory additions in the 1960s (fluoride), by insufficient subtractions in the 1990s (Thames Water Plc's 'effluent on tap'), and finally transmuted into Perrier, the multinational *eau de vie*.

It is vignettes such as this that link Wright's twin themes. *Journey Through Ruins* is partly about the enormous power of landscape as a repository of people's memories and values, and its consequent vulnerability to appropriation and exploitation of all kinds. It is also about the meanings and hopes embedded in public institutions, and *their* vulnerability. Together, they make the sub-plot of 'The Last Days of London' an enquiry into the last days of a truly common visual language.

Patrick Wright is fortunate as a writer (and, I suspect, as a citizen) in living in Dalston Lane, one of England's authentic back rows and a track that burrows through the strata of centuries of immigration and cultural shifts. He makes his walks down it sound almost like nature rambles, emphasising how superficial the division between 'rural' and 'urban' is at the cultural grass roots. On the East Side, so to speak, there are remnants of the 'deep England' of craft, duty and, occasionally, deference. Pizzey's High Class Florists from the 1950s; a network of Victorian workshops still buzzing with tailors, antique restorers, violin makers; the mix of Georgian and Baroque architecture in Kendalls undertakers, where 'an ancient glass sign over the door still promises "Funeral Feathermen and Carriage Masters"'. On the symbolic West Side is the typically modern mix of rampant monetarism and New Gothic: the windowless fortress of Dalston police station (empty since 1990 when the force withdrew to their new 'supernick' in Stoke Newington, where guided tours are offered of the 'cell suites'); Pamela's restaurant, done up with stylish ironwork and a gallery and offering 'a taste of the Caribbean, a hint of French cuisine'.

Running through both quarters is another elemental thread: dirt. Blight and squalor have been facts of life for centuries in old Hackney. But what one might call 'squalor in the head' has, for the new bourgeoisie, become not much more than a fashion accessory to stress the blue-chip earthiness of their recent settlements. 'Upwardly mobile debris' Wright calls it in one of his deliciously understated, Martian phrases. The 'New Baroque sensibility' is everywhere: in the grainy black-and-white photos on the advertising hoardings, in Peter Ackroyd's Gothic fictions, in the TV film crews queuing up to use Hackney's derelict and echoing locations. It is a 'lurid appetite for a Gin Lane *frisson*' that is in sharpest contrast to a real appreciation of the variegated lives and landscapes different cultural groups have created here.

But the crumbling local infrastructure and its inhabitants weren't always so casually exploited. During the Blitz, an earlier set of East End ruins was explored by artists like John Minton and Graham Sutherland, looking for inspiration in the rubble. They found it, like 'a condition of grace', in the people's responses and temper. The critic Viola Garvin, writing of Wanda Ostrowska's watercolours, described the ruins of the city as 'pediments of solidity' on which 'the newly steeled spirit of the nation could rest'. Wright adds a crucial comment: 'The first blitz produced a spirit of solidarity and common interest that was built into the Welfare State; the second is an aesthetic effect found in the ruins of that reforming endeavour.' 'Common interest' is itself now viewed as a rather quaint piece of emotional junk. But before the war it formed the basis of a radical alternative to those bleakly opposed forces of development and privileged conservation. Wright's local mansion is Sutton House, a grade II listed building dating from 1500, and now owned by the National Trust. In recent years it has fallen into a familiar state of decay, and the National Trust had drawn up plans to convert it into a suite of five private flats. It was one of the leaders of the local opposition to this threatened act of appropriation who unearthed a remarkable piece of history in Hackney's archives. One of the signatories to a 1930s appeal to save Sutton House for local community use was George Lansbury – East End MP, leader of the Labour Party, pacifist, supporter of women's rights and, extraordinarily by modern expectations, a Vice President of the National Trust. Lansbury himself, though, saw no contradictions in his affiliations, nor between conservation and social reform.

What such policies presaged have always been too much for those irretrievably rooted in deep England. In 1941 James Lees Milne glimpsed the vulgarity to come, and felt that 'architecture and the continuity of history . . . were living, palpable children to me. They and the man-fashioned landscape outside were the England that mattered. I suddenly saw them as infinitely fragile and precious. They meant to me then, and have meant to me since, far more than human lives. They represent the things of the spirit. And the ghastly thing is that like humans they are not perdurable.'

Yet Brideshead's furnishings and fittings have proved astonishingly durable – albeit by changing their meanings and associations. Much of the debris of 'The Treasure Houses of Britain' has been shipped across the Atlantic, there to form the basis of the latest Ralph Lauren 'lifestyle marketing' under the slogan 'How a Tradition Becomes'. East-coast young fogeys, the *New York Times* reports, 'see home as a haven in which they can be themselves, surrounded by the broken-in comfort of proved classic quality'.

Meanwhile, back in London's East End, what the *Telegraph*'s man called 'the Nighthawks' are making their claims to a slice of the 'continuity of history' on moonless nights out on the Thames mudflats. It was an inspired stroke by Wright to include a chapter on 'The Man with a Metal Detector' and he ventures into the detectorists' masonic world like a cub war-reporter running with his first guerrilla band. He comes from a culture that views the detectorists as modern Goths and Vandals, bent on looting the national heritage. Yet he finds in them a romantic passion for history and the kind of self-taught craft-knowledge (if not the respect for commonwealth) that William Morris espoused: 'The detector's world is set off against the abstract uniformities of the modern state. It is a landscape of atmospheres, ancient recognitions, and places that have uniquely different qualities: it is full of old continuities resumed.'

Objects – and landscapes-with-objects – continue to play their complex roles as totems and taboos, property and blessing, till the close of the book. Wright contrasts Theo Crosby's megalomaniac plans for a Battle of Britain monument in the heart of Dockland with the views of the original citizens of that benighted area (who still call it defiantly 'the Isle of Dogs'). Crosby's version – by Wagner out of Alfred Watkins – is of a giant granite-clad pyramid, aligned along London ley lines and bizarre 'cultural axes' (based on a kind of divination of Canaletto and Turner paintings), and full of images that 'come whisperingly to life on arrival and die away as the visitor leaves': underground shelters, barrage balloons, chairs and a table set with 'a simple meal, a corpse laid out', a Heinkel bomber crashing through a disintegrating cathedral. Fortunately the impertinent monstrosity is still on the drawing board, and those locals who have stuck it out on the Isle continue to regard their wartime memories as rather more than ephemeral and patronising whispers. Scraps of landscape still speak to them, individually, of that massive, communal experience: air-raid shelter remains, rope-walks, happenstance ponds, a few initials carved in concrete in 1940, and the Mudchute, north of Milwall Park, where mud dredged from the docks was dumped in the nineteenth century, and where there were 400 allotments up to the 1950s. Above all this there hover continually those avenging, cleansing angels, Conversion and Restoration, offering to replace all these unhygienic mementoes with a heliport or holiday village; or, better still, an historical theme park where they could all be remade in back-lit pre-cast concrete, with added Spitfire sound-tracks. Fortunately this is one instance where local residents won the day, and the Mudchute, complete with its anti-aircraft emplacements (Big Ada and Big Nelly), has been saved as a city farm. So, 'for most visitors the emplacements can disappear entirely into the modesty of their new function as pig pens and goat sheds, but others can still come here for secret and entirely untravestied communication with the remembered events of the war'.

Patrick Wright speaks for his fellow Dalstonians with compassion, humour, irony and a wonderfully original vision. (His chapter in defence of the old red phone box as a truly democratic landscape feature, a fusion between classic design and public service, is a maverick masterpiece.) If, at first reading, he has one fault, it is a slight detachment. This is a perennial pitfall when analysing landscape, which after all started with the Claude glass, where you stood on an eminence with your back to the scene and contemplated its unalloyed, uncontexted reflection. Wright never turns his back on the landscape and you know precisely where he stands; yet occasionally he seems to be contemplating his neighbourhood not from street level but from a second-floor balcony in Mapledene's mid-Victorian terraces, a safe, concrete block's throw from the Holly Street Estate.

But on second thoughts this is exactly where a writer should be, if he so chooses. The point of Wright's book is precisely to challenge that tired 1980s dogma that public landscapes (and institutions) are necessarily monumental and monocultural. *A Journey Through Ruins* is a celebration of cultural pluralism and the distinctiveness of place, an imaginative projection into an urban setting of the ancient concept of *commonland*. Above all it insists that those who deal in landscape – be it houses or 'housing', object or art object – must have the profoundest respect for the meanings which the physical stuff of the land holds for ordinary people.

1991

Eric Ashby

Like millions of other viewers, I first became aware of Eric Ashby on a January night in 1961, when his spellbinding film *The Unknown Forest* was shown on BBC television, and in forty-five minutes permanently changed the standards for home-grown wildlife documentaries. Anyone raised on modern natural history films may find it hard to appreciate the impact made by this intimate look into the lives of our native animals. For much of the 1950s wildlife documentary had been dominated by glamorous globetrotting naturalists like Armand and Michaela Denis. Their films were fast-moving, exotic, superbly photographed, but presented a picture of nature as something remote and romantic – and the animals themselves, on occasions, as little more than free-range circus performers.

By the side of these, Eric Ashby's quiet, respectful cameos of foxes and badgers were a revelation. They had an austere dignity and a vivid sense of place. Most of the details of the film have faded from my memory, but I have a sharp recollection of its mood, of its contrast of early-morning light and dappled shade, of animals held simply but enthrallingly in the centre of the frame, of an amiably decrepit backcloth that could only have been an ancient English wood.

It was difficult, that year, to consider Eric's work separately from the revolutions that were happening in other areas of documentary in the cinema and on radio, and their common moves towards the recording of local culture and ordinary experience. Ashby himself also seemed to belong to the new mood. He was unassuming to a fault, committed to working in the place where he lived, and showed no taste for the glamorous life of the professional film-maker. Not long after *The Unknown Forest* was first screened he was christened 'the silent watcher'; and a glimpse of his shadowy figure, crouched by a tree, yards from an intrigued fox or deer (a small Hitchcockian indulgence in several of his films) was about all the public ever saw of him. Few people realised then what a body of hard work and hard-won wisdom lay behind his unobtrusive, almost donnish exterior. Eric had been making nature films since 1935, when he was only seventeen, and had taken his first still photograph – a terrier nosing at a hedgehog – five years before that. Even in those early days he was under the spell of the New Forest, and in 1953 put down permanent roots in a cottage on its western edge. Since then he has built up an incomparable photo-graphic record of its creatures, landscapes, seasonal moods and moments of sadness. He has become recognised as the champion of the Forest's wildlife, and his pictures are not so much detached scientific records as portraits – the animals' best shots.

Even from the quickest of scans it is clear that his still photo-graphs share many of the qualities of his films. There is a winning modesty about them, a sense that the subject is more important than the photographer and his stylistic niceties. They are full of the kind of insights that come from long and patient contemplation of that mysterious other existence of animals.

Yet what shines through is not nature's 'otherness' at all, but its generosity and lack of malice, the harmony that ultimately transcends its often disturbing and violent surface details. It is no insult to Eric's technical skill to say that his stills collection is, in a sense, a family album as well as a naturalist's portfolio. The pictures – even the most light-hearted ones – evoke many different levels of feeling about our relationships with animals. Recently Eric and his wife Eileen have been devoting much of their energies to rehabilitating injured and abandoned foxes and, in one picture, an obviously recuperated orphan has been caught standing on its hind legs behind a camera and seemingly peering through the viewfinder at Eric. It is good postcard comedy, with just a touch of forgivable sentimentality. Yet for such bright and insatiably curious mammals (they already muck in with the domestic round at Badger Cottage) it isn't really such an outlandish or contrived scene. It is the kind of prank a wild fox might pull, if anyone left a camera standing in a field. And at a more serious level, it is a reminder that Eric's portraits also hint at the views animals hold of *us*. There are few of his images in which some kind of human presence – benign, puzzling, barbarous on occasions – is not implied or reflected.

Eric has never felt tempted to work much beyond the New Forest boundaries (though I suspect his rapport with animals would be the same in Africa or Amazonia), and he may be one of those naturalists, like Gilbert White, whose sensibilities are deepened when they are deliberately confined within an intimately known locality. It would certainly be hard to think of any region of Britain more suited to his particular outlook and talents. The New Forest is a huge and eccentric anomaly, a refuge from the pervasive tameness of much of southern England, yet a place where humans and animals have lived convivially for centuries. It is the most popular wooded playground in the country, yet has almost nothing in common with the neat and pocket-sized landscapes which are supposed to epitomise our rural heritage. It is in a state of almost permanent siege – split by a dual carriageway whose creation was a national disgrace, and squeezed by Southampton's industrial complexes to the east and Bournemouth's ribbon development to the west – yet it still hangs on doggedly as the largest patch of uncultivated lowland in north-west Europe.

Eric Ashby began coming to this liberating place when he was a child. He was born in 1918 on the west coast of Cumberland, and spent all his early years in the countryside, including a spell in Lymington close to the Forest boundary. When he was ten, his parents decided on a move to Southsea, for the sake of their children's schooling, and it was here, in 1930, that Eric attended a lecture by the pioneer film-maker and naturalist Cherry Kearton. From that moment Eric began to dream of making his own photographic record of wildlife in natural habitats. He had already acquired his first camera, an old-style mahogany model, whose plates had to be developed and printed at home. By the time he was sixteen he was taking accomplished photographs of birds. The *Boy's Own Paper* for August 1935 carries Eric's first published work, an article written and illustrated by him: 'Bird Photography – An Ideal Hobby'. It has notes on the building of hides, and strict instructions about returning nest-sites to the conditions in which they were found.

His real ambitions lay in moving pictures, and later that year he managed to save enough money – £6 10s – to buy a second-hand 16mm Ensign camera. Soon he was filming house-martins on the Isle of Wight. But it was to be another twenty-five years before Eric's films received any kind of recognition. Before that, in 1932, Eric's father died. He had suspected that farming was the only suitable occupation for his countryside-loving sons, and the family, still thinking in terms of a farming future, moved temporarily into a cottage on the edge of the New Forest while they searched for an affordable holding. But there was nothing suitable locally, and in 1939 they settled for a property in Devon. It was an eighty-six-acre mixed farm with stock, corn, potatoes and vegetables, and, to Eric's delight (he had photographed his first badger before leaving the Forest), both a badger sett and a fox earth. It also had 500 free-range poultry, and Eric recalls with some pride that, thanks to his understanding of animal behaviour, they did not lose a single bird to foxes during fourteen years of farming.

In 1953 Eric returned to the New Forest, settled at Linwood, and began accumulating the footage that was to form the basis of *The Unknown Forest*. Badgers, a passion ever since he had heard as a boy about the cruelties of badger-baiting, were his favourite subject, and his early pictures of them were an extraordinary achievement. They were exposed in daylight with a home-made kapok 'blimp' to dull the noise of the camera, and were almost certainly the first films to be made of badgers in the wild.

Eric's breakthrough happened almost by chance in 1958. The

BBC's Natural History Unit in Bristol were anxious to broaden the scope and appeal of their programmes, and were casting about for indigenous film-makers with a potential for reaching a mass audience. A producer had read an article by Eric in the *Countryman* magazine, and travelled down to the Forest to view his material. So it was that in October of that year Chris Parsons, later head of the Unit, sat in a viewing room in Bristol, transfixed by the first close-up pictures he or anyone else had seen of wild badgers digging, playing and feeding. Eric was given a contract immediately, and spent 1959 filming additional sequences. *The Unknown Forest* was screened on 19 January 1961, and had an overwhelming public response.

Over the years that followed Eric made a score of films for the BBC, all photographed in southern England, and most of them concentrating on the New Forest and its large mammals. In these, as in his still pictures, he has worked to an unwavering set of principles. He has never faked continuity to create a better story-line, or used tame animals posing as wild ones. He has never resorted to trick photography, and refers dismissively to some modern initiatives in this direction as '*un*-natural history films'. Instead Eric relies on intuition, patience and sheer fieldcraft, sometimes tracking animals downwind for hours before setting up his camera. Ever since his first foray in *Boy's Own Paper* he has insisted that the welfare of his subjects comes first. He told me of the time he was filming a nesting Dartford warbler, one of Britain's rarest resident bird species, which has a last precarious stronghold on the Forest heaths. He allowed himself one hour in the hide (a long time for a bird but short for a photographer), while his wife Eileen sat in a parked car nearby, flicking ostentatiously through the pages of a book to distract passers-by.

Eric's perseverance has been rewarded with a remarkable collection of insights into the lives of ordinary creatures, and with glimpses of a world where the barrier between humans and nature has, for a moment, been lowered. One of his most endearing pictures is of a group of three mammals consorting in the garden of Badger Cottage. There is Eric himself, remote-control shutter in hand; the immense and imperturbable cat, Ginger, a stray who had taken up residence in the garden's badger sett; and, emerging from the sett itself a few yards away, a wild badger.

Eric's art is essentially that of a story-teller. Although many of his Forest landscapes are striking compositions, what makes his animal pictures so compelling is the hint of past and future events uncoiling from them. Like all fine photographs they do not 'freeze' time so much as admit its passing. And an important part of their narrative concerns Eric's relationship with his subjects. Many of his strongest portraits show animals looking directly at the camera – and not always because they are unaware of it. Such pictures capture that special moment when a human and a wild creature have accepted each other's presence.

In 1975 Eric began building an artificial badger sett in his garden, so that he could have better opportunities to film the animals at close quarters. (It's now nicknamed 'the film sett'.) This is as close as he has ever come to intervening in his subjects' lives.

It was a complicated project. He excavated a series of trenches about eighty yards from the natural sett on the edge of his lawn and filled them with wide concrete pipes to act as tunnels. They led to a glass-fronted chamber under the garden shed. Many months later a family of badgers moved in, and Eric – gradually accustoming them to artificial light – was able to take the first-ever film of wild mammals underground. There was no interference with the badgers' lifestyles beyond the provision of a few pounds of scraps every day.

In 1987 Eric was preparing to make another film based on the badgers, which had now started to breed in the artificial sett. But early that year his property was invaded by the local foxhunt. The hounds ran riot across his garden, pounding the soft edges of the natural sett entrances, and causing all the badgers (including the pregnant females) to desert. Eric has always opposed the activities of the three New Forest Hunts. But on this occasion they had violated not only his feelings but the relationship he had been building with a specific family of badgers over many years, and he decided to apply for an injunction forbidding foxhunts to trespass on his two-and-a-half acres.

It was a brave act, made at some personal cost. The case attracted much publicity and the attention of pro-hunt extremists. Eric began to receive anonymous communications. One night he found his garage had been broken into, and a dead fox with its face smashed in lying on his lawn. In January 1988, when the badger family started to move back, someone drenched the sett with Renardine, an agricultural chemical used to repel foxes and badgers from chicken runs, but which is supposedly regarded as unethical by the hunting community. Again, the badgers deserted.

There is no evidence that the New Forest Hunts were involved in any of these witless acts of vandalism. But after Eric had successfully applied for his injunction, they chose a curious way of complying. Instead of simply declaring his property out of bounds (the usual procedure), they built a permanent, six-foot-high, animal-proof fence along 300 yards of his northern boundary. On hunting days an electric fence is strung along most of the rest. The fences keep the hounds out, but also most of the other wild animals that used to share Badger Cottage, including a herd of fallow deer which, Eric says, 'used to feed on our land every day, often lying down in front of our windows'. The fence was erected by local hunt members, and *Hounds* magazine, thanking the 'ever-faithful band of Footfloggers', christened it 'stage one of Stalag Ashby'.

I thought of this tasteless analogy as I sat in the garden of Badger Cottage on an autumn afternoon, romping with the orphan foxes and marvelling at how Eric had kept his tolerant outlook in the face of such provocation. Later I wandered out into the Forest. I thought about the grim symbolism of that fence around Badger Cottage, and realised more acutely than ever before how much I (and all lovers of the New Forest, I suspect) treasured the sense of having free run of such a vast area of wild country. It was a day made for walking, with a soft breeze coming off the sea. I picked my way through damp valleys where the air was scented with bog myrtle, glimpsed a kingfisher darting through a tunnel

143

of blackberries over Linford Brook, and scrambled about among an immense willow brought down in the 1987 gale, already bristling with new shoots along the whole length of its trunk.

Serendipity comes easily here. On a high heath near Bolderwood I was looking out towards the unfenced woods of Bushy Bratley when I saw a pert, dusky-plumaged warbler darting about between the gorse clumps. It flicked its tail up on landing and even from a distance I could make out its flanks shining the colour of heather flowers in the sun. It was a Dartford warbler, the species which Eric had photographed on the nest all those years ago, now the Forest's rarest small bird and the first I had ever seen. They are usually the shyest of birds, but, true to the spirit of the place that day, this one sported about in the open for a full quarter of an hour. Through my binoculars I could see its brilliant red eye and steel-grey back. And I saw one other extraordinary thing: the air between us was full of strings of translucent gossamer, and the warbler was feasting on money spiders dangling out of the sky.

My thanks go out to Eric for that day. He has helped educate the eyes and sensibilities of all of us, and in this corner of England has been a stalwart defender of the wild creatures themselves. What the New Forest – and Eric's celebrations of it – demonstrates is the power of wild creatures to elevate and inform the human spirit; and the possibility of a contract between humans, nature and the land.

1988

Tony Evans

A couple of months ago I was browsing over a dilapidated map of the Cotswolds when I noticed a scatter of faintly pencilled plant names between the mud stains. 'Alkanet' and 'Dame's violet' hovered above the villages between Barton and Lower Slaughter. 'May' was ringed in thick circles over half a square mile of hillside near Winchcombe. I suddenly realised it was the map Tony Evans and I had shared on one of our plant-hunting expeditions, marked up with sites for Tony to visit with his camera later. And in a trice I could remember every detail of that spring foray – the drifts of escaped alkanet dotting the village lanesides; the one perfect clump we found against a dry-stone wall, with its clear blue flowers caught up in lacy nets of fading cow parsley; and the hill called Belas Knapp, from which we scanned the billowing rows of hawthorn blossom – H. E. Bates's 'risen cream of May-time' – marking out the contour lines and field boundaries.

Tony died of cancer in the spring of 1992, having almost single-handedly rescued plant photography from the Dark Ages. I knew him as a dear friend, and we spent six summers on the road together, working on our cultural history of wild plants, *The Flowering of Britain*. It was a transforming experience for me – a voyage of discovery of my home country, a first taste of the joys of fieldwork, and above all a process of learning and exchange about different ways of looking at the natural world.

We had met exactly twenty years previously. I was a tyro writer, fresh from *Food For Free*, and Tony, a few years older than I, was already one of the most distinguished figures in commercial photography, famous for his meticulousness, his weakness for gadgets, his immense expenses bills and his anarchic sense of humour. His *Radio Times* cover photo for the Royal Variety Performance – a corgi emerging from a top hat – is still one of the best photographic jokes. But he was restless, and longed to do more meaningful and intellectually rewarding work.

It was the editor of *Nova* magazine who brought us together, to collaborate on a feature on the troubled fortunes of our wild flowers. Tony came over with his wife, Caroline, to discuss the project with me in the early spring. We hit it off from the outset, and by the end of the day I was confiding to him my dream of a book that would go beyond the *Nova* feature, and celebrate in words and pictures the role which wild plants had played in our human and physical landscape.

Within a couple of weeks Tony had been on a trip to the wild daffodil country round Dymock in Gloucestershire, and brought back an astonishing portfolio of pictures. They were unlike any wild-flower photographs I had seen before. The daffodils rippled in deep focus over the floor of an ancient oak coppice, buoyed up the walls of a medieval church, jostled along trackways and boundary banks. It was as if Tony's film was sensitive not just to light, but to all the historical and ecological resonances of a place. And in one study, which troubled me initially because of its unashamed revelling in the sheer *look* of the plants, he had filled the frame with a whole troop, animated, glowing, all facing the same way – Wordsworth's dancing host to a T.

I was confident we could do the book together, yet I think I initially envied the initiative and insight that had helped him find the core of the daffodil's character so quickly. (I had not yet even *seen* a wild daffodil.) I rationalised the feeling as a worry that he might be too much in awe of pure composition. He doubtless found my over-intellectual view as to what constituted a 'good' plant picture equally worrying, not to say impertinent.

146

That slight tension between our respective ways of looking at the natural world came to the surface on our first field trip together a few weeks later. We'd travelled to the Bradfield Woods in Suffolk, to try for oxlips. But the auguries weren't good. The oxlips were past their best and thinner on the ground than usual. I was embarrassed at getting the dates wrong, and made all kinds of excuses for myself, for the plant, for the whole philosophy of the book. When we did find a clump big and fresh enough to warrant a picture, I was hugely relieved, and considered that my contribution to the process was finished. I was all for moving on and finding something else, a wild pear tree or herb paris, perhaps. With a head full of romantic ideas about plants as symbols and indicators, the mere presence of the oxlips seemed sufficient for me.

But not for Tony. He insisted that I sat still and explained to him what we *needed* from this plant. And as we talked, he began to assemble his own vision of this oxlip, not just as a member of a species with an ecological history, but as a unique and particular individual, with its own character and its own relations with the light, the weather, its neighbours and this moment in the wood. It was a perspective which sowed in me a new awareness of the immediacy and vitality of plants, and which shines through in Tony's finished oxlip picture. A clump of more than a dozen flower spikes rises like a sheaf, ungardened and luxuriant, in the left foreground. It is tangled up with dead twigs, young meadowsweet leaves and the flaying stalks of tussock grass. Behind it, caught by a wide-angle lens, the ancient coppice shears away towards the sky. The oxlips aren't just in the wood, they are *of* it.

We spent the next six springs and summers exploring places like this, always trying to discover scenes that showed plants in their ecological and cultural contexts. In the flat reaches of the Norfolk Broads we stalked fenland species from a boat, trying to catch the weaving and windiness of the lush vegetation. In the highlands of western Argyll we failed dismally to reach any true alpines but found mountain plants growing at sea level on the balmy west coast, on a day so hot that we both spent much of the time under Tony's pink photographic parasol. We pored over Suffolk estate maps tracing Saxon boundaries that were still marked by pollard elms and poplars. And in Westmorland we walked gingerly over the sun-baked and glacier-scoured limestone pavements of Underbarrow Scar, marvelling at plants that seemed to be growing out of bare rock. We seemed to be blessed by perpetual sunshine in those summers of the mid-1970s, and I remember resting between the dwarf junipers and bloody cranesbills on that north-western trip to eat wild strawberries which had been turned into melting beads of sweetness by the heat.

During the height of the flowering season we lived like a couple of botanical gypsies. We travelled and worked from Tony's Dormobile, which was stocked not just with dozens of aluminium cases of equipment and a comprehensive botanical library, but hoards of the kinds of gadgets Tony found irresistible: an altimeter to tell when it was worth searching for alpines, ski-stick ends to support tripod legs on boggy ground, his famous custom-built portable wind-tents, electronic (and quite useless) mosquito repellents.

One summer evening in Sussex we chanced on some glow-worms near our hotel. Tony stayed up late taking time exposures of them, having found that their diminutive lamps registered on his specialist Weston lightmeter.

Fortuitousness of this kind was a feature of our trips. There were tip-offs in pubs and unexpected vistas glimpsed in the driving mirror. In Oxford we found Oxford ragwort growing in a glass-strewn waste patch in front of a line of posters advertising the arrival of the circus in Oxford. (And only Tony had the charm to explain to an increasingly resentful band of local denizens and winos why his camera was pointed towards the gents convenience all day.)

Yet if there was serendipity, there was also routine of a kind. Joe Cocker tapes to keep Tony awake when he was at the wheel. Long picnic lunches, with cheap white wine (river-cooled, if we were lucky), over which we would hold Socratic debates about the progress of the project and the rest of the day's work. I think

148

that after a couple of years we had learned a good deal from each other. I had started to come out of my archival shell where plants were chiefly signs and landmarks, and begun to revel a bit more sensuously in the wild thyme. Tony, for his part, was absorbing the idea that plants had landscape and historical contexts, and was beginning to express this in the most subtle of ways. His portrait of five marsh marigold flowers peeping between the gnarled roots of an ancient tree stump is strangely evocative of a great ecological crisis six millennia ago, when the climate chilled and wettened and the great forests began to decline, but it never becomes a dull lecture slide.

Yet even when we were working most closely, I like to think that we found and respected the limits of our different skills: writing, an organised, narrative but essentially abstract business that hopefully reaches out towards the specific; and photography, rooted in moment and particularity, but striving towards general statements.

It is easy to forget what plant photography was like in the 1960s. There were landscape pictures and, always separate, there were close-ups, usually flash-lit or taken against contrast screens. They had the look of plants in glass cases, devoid of growth and setting and atmosphere. Tony never used a flash in his wild-flower photography, and barely ever arranged his subject for a 'better' shot. Instead he would spend hours – sometimes days – looking for an example that would, *in itself*, say everything that we both wanted to convey. He used trees as backcloths to isolate a single bloom from a mass (as in his bluebell picture from Dorset). He relied on the complications of leaves in hedgebanks and woods to provide the depth and shading in his pictures – exactly as they did in an ecosystem. His field poppy – probably the best known of all his pictures – is a brilliant example of the use of focus to convey time. I had rather hoped to have poppies glowing amongst golden corn, but Tony had glimpsed something much less clichéd – that the whole cycle and texture of a poppy's life could be contained in a single picture. In sharp focus are the fully open flowers and seed-heads (one entwined by black bindweed). In the foreground engorged buds droop, while at the rear, out-of-focus flowers – floppy, translucent, like 'painted glass' as Ruskin suggested – merge into a dappled mist of green stalks.

His patience and persistence were extraordinary. His portrait of the historic pollard elms in the village of Knapwell, Cambridgeshire, took a week of customised weather forecasts and at least four day-trips to the site. Tony wanted (and eventually got) a thin, early-morning mist, a natural gauze filter that would emphasise the elms' monumental quality and hint at both their antiquity and their uncertain future. The unplanned feature was the white horse that posed with almost Arthurian resonance amongst the trees.

We did not always get such good results. In 1974 we were in the Derbyshire Dales, nosing around. It was another baking day, and climbing up towards Lathkill Dale Tony suddenly stopped, pulled the scissors out of his immense rucksack of equipment and said, 'Cut my legs off, Rich.' Later we found an extraordinary colony of columbines, both blue and white, growing on a steep slope, and Tony, now wearing nothing but his newly beshortened jeans, set to work under the fierce sun. He stayed in the same spot for the next six hours, and I watched him with increasing anxiety, as he rotated slowly round the columbines like a sundial's shadow (or maybe like a heliotrope: I always felt at times like this that Tony *became* the plant). But the picture didn't work. The columbines looked gangly and parched, sticking out of the short grass on the hill. I understand why now, since they are really woodland plants, and, as Tony always insisted, you cannot photograph what is not there.

But we had our best times among limestone plants and landscapes. They had a frankness and vivacity that suited us both. Near Shap, not really knowing what we were looking for, we tracked down bird's-eye primroses on the very dome of the fells, in grassland shining honey and silvery under the late June sun. And in the Burren in County Clare, during our long stay in 1977, Tony took perhaps his most evocative picture, of burnet roses around a flat limestone rock. In the rock is a puddle, like a tiny turlough, and on its dead-calm surface a reflection of the sun is surrounded by white rose petals. It is a picture of the whole Burren in miniature.

When Tony died I was going through a bad patch of my own, regretting a life that seemed too small and solitary. Grieving forced me to remember those times we had together, the unique experiences we shared and I hope communicated to others, and most of all the exhilaration of knowing him as a friend and as an apostle for the living. His last words to me, when I enquired anxiously about his health just weeks before his death, were, '*Today*, I am very well.' Now, whenever I sense depression or cynicism or over-intellectualism stealing up, I recall Tony's sheer delight at a single dandelion flower in a plain green field.

This June in the Burren I think I found the exact spot where he took his burnet-rose picture. It was as hauntingly beautiful as ever but, needless to say, totally different from Tony's picture – which remains a triumphant record of a unique, unrepeatable moment that no one can take away.

1993

Don McCullin

When he was five years old, Don McCullin, the doyen of war photographers, was evacuated to Somerset, and imprinted by a pastoral England drowsy with blossom and Arthurian echoes. Half a century later and spiritually exhausted by the daily sight of human corpses and bomb-wrecked land, he has been stalking the fields round Glastonbury again, searching for that lost domain. His solace, he explains, 'lies in recording what remains of the beautiful landscape of Somerset and its metallic dark skies'. *Open Skies* is his photographic elegy to those remains.

McCullin is a haunted man. Images of starving Biafrans and shell-shocked GIs still 'ferment in my darker self' and cast a shadow over his landscape pictures. This collection is full of elemental Somerset scenes – distant swans in the empty Levels, the sweeps of dairy country below the Tors and Roman temples, tangled ditches, flooded cart-tracks. But they are dark, depopulated, trapped in winter. Far from reflecting the 'open skies' of the title, they cower under oppressive cloud. Louring cumuli seep like bloodstains above the horizon of 'The real English countryside, Somerset, 1988'. The Dorset borderlands seem to tilt under the force of a hailstorm.

This is a faithful, albeit relentless, view of a kind of countryside not often admitted in the tourist brochures. As John Fowles suggests in his Introduction, it is less a view of east Somerset than of a state of mind, 'the subjective reflection of an uneasy spirit'. And

Fowles stresses another undercurrent of meaning in these bleak prospects. McCullin has not really given up war photography at all, but is now recording that 'most terrible and senseless conflict . . . between man and his own environment'.

This is a weighty project for photography to bear. Symbolism can easily collapse into contrivance or melodrama (I hope 'Peaceful fields under threat of development' – in which a chequerboard Somerset lies beneath a cloud of such fearful symmetry that all it lacks is heraldic avenging angels – is intended as a joke). Realism can fade into ambivalence from, ironically, its sheer intimacy, its lack of history and context. In 'Burnham-on-Sea, with the dreaded Hinkley Point Power Station in background', the dreaded pile, lit up by a shaft of sunlight in the distance, looks as innocent as a happenstance boulder. In 'The unacceptable face of bad land management', the fertiliser bags and debris strewn around a dyke have, in the leaden light, the look of huge windblown leaves.

In all this gloom it is impossible not to be reminded of John Ruskin's depression in the 1870s, when he became convinced he could detect a black storm-cloud stationed over the country [see page 172]. He described its effects as 'blanched sun – blighted grass – blinded man', and said he felt 'disconsolate . . . as if it was no use fighting for a world any more in which there could be no sunrise'. This was the despair of a man who had lost his faith not just in a human reconciliation with nature, but in nature itself.

There is something of the same hopelessness in McCullin's Somerset photographs. It is not that they are monotonous or morbid – indeed there is a compelling, almost runic fascination about them – but that they are indiscriminate. In the end, their obsessive, dark motif dominates and levels out the vitality of nature almost as surely as the forces it is directed against.

One conspicuous exception is 'Wintry morning sun', a fieldscape much of whose foreground is occupied by a bramble patch. It is hunched and bristly, like a Green Man or an ancient sea-urchin that is about to be warmed back into life by the rising sun. It is an oddly cheering picture, and it may be no coincidence that it is the only one to have a close and sympathetically observed detail rather than generalised background scenery – just the kind of feature that gives even the most harrowing of McCullin's war photographs their sense of hope and humanity.

1989

Art and Ecology

Goethe's artist Young Werther, in one of his less tragic moods, believed that it might be possible to understand the mysteries of existence if only he could lose himself in nature, at its literal grass roots: 'When I lie in the tall grass and, closer thus to the earth, become conscious of the thousand varieties of little plants; when I feel the swarming of all that diminutive world among the blades . . . when I feel these closer to my heart, and feel the presence of the Almighty who created us in His image . . . then how often, longingly, do I say to myself: "Ah! if you could but express, if you could but bring to life again on paper, the feeling that pulses so richly, so warmly within you, so that it might become the mirror of your soul." '

Seeking heaven – or at least revelation – in a wild flower, hoping to comprehend or portray the universe through its 'minute particulars', has been one of the fundamental impulses of ecologically tinged art. Behind it is a belief that there is some kind of unity in nature, and that the complicated patterns and associations of the whole are echoed, or crystallised, in its smallest fragments.

This assumption has been the gathering ground for all kinds of holistic creeds, from the toughly political to florid New Age paganism. Yet increasingly they have science on their side. Modern biology is more and more inclined to see organisms and their environments as whole entities. One does not have to be an out and out Gaian these days to accept that all living things are linked through the great commonweals of air and water. Or that evolution might have proceeded not just by the repeated outstripping of the poorly adapted by the fit and flexible, but by all kinds of marriages of convenience, symbioses and combinations. Even our own cells can no longer be appropriated as our private property. We are, as the biologist Lewis Thomas has written, 'shared, rented, occupied'. The interior of our cells is a cooperative of minute, independent creatures that swam together for mutual convenience aeons ago, and stayed that way. The picture of the cell community increasingly resembles one of those hybrid, mythological life forms – the griffin, sphinx, centaur, and the like – with which the world's bestiaries are full, and which seem to reflect an intuitive understanding that the evolution of life on earth has been a matter of cooperation as well as competition.

Modern biology is full to bursting with artistic resonance and mythic power, yet it seems barely to have shown its head in the current debate about the relationship between science and art. The arguments have been preoccupied with the teachings of modern physics and the psychology of perception, and have an arid, reductionist feel about them. Both sides seem, paradoxically, to be locked into an antiquely dualistic world. There is Art and there is Nature. There is an Artist and an Art Object and a Viewer, having – though more often it sounds like consuming – Aesthetic Experiences, shaped by either deep neural structures or abstract principles.

But is this the end of it? Can't artistic transactions also be untidy, diffuse, mutable? Aren't they often explorations of ideas, expressions of instinctive outrage, passages of pure play as much as divinations of structural beauty? And isn't one of the clearest analogies of artistic activity the protean business of biological evolution itself?

Any art which is open to these kinds of ideas is already beginning to be biologically sensitive. Ecology is a more complicated matrix, as it has, in popular understanding at least, a moral as well

156

as a descriptive component. An art informed by ecology would reflect holistic views and consciously try to harmonise its own processes with those of the natural world. The flow of images and ideas between the disciplines would also be two-way, with the art helping to illuminate and criticise the science, to highlight its ethical dilemmas and insights, every bit as much as the reverse.

The vision of a harmonious creation has been one of the universal grails of art. Young Werther's dream itself had been perfectly, if pedantically, realised two-and-a-half centuries earlier by his fellow countryman Dürer. In *Large Tuft of Herbs*, Dürer created an exquisitely detailed portrait of a single square foot of grassland, in which the most remarkable feature is not so much the liveliness and accuracy of the individual plants as the fact that they are patently contributing to each other's lives. The dandelions and plantains are flowering, bending, propping each other up, finding their niches, fading and seeding, living in both time and space.

Today the picture has the look of a vivid and accomplished botanical illustration, ecological with a small e. But in 1503 it presupposed a view of nature as an autonomous, complex and mutually supportive creation that was 200 years ahead of its time.

Landscape painting has had a long fascination with holism – since at least the fourteenth century, when the early Italian calendar studies portrayed whole environments at precise moments of the year, complete with their seasonal crops and working peasants. Visions of an interdependent nature appear in the most surprising places, in surrealism and magic realism for instance. Henri Rousseau's invented jungles, for all their fantastic plastic blossoms and neatly pruned trees, have a compelling sense of rightness and mutuality. They *work*. And even the bleakest of Paul Nash's wartime landscapes (*Totes Meer*, for example, with the wrecked planes metamorphosing into sand-dunes) seem to offer the possibility of resilient regrowth from the chaos.

But though such works catch glimpses of a holistic world, one huge unanswered question stands out from all of them. Where do *we*, as humans, stand in relation to these scenes, to the exterior world of nature? Where, more specifically, does the artist stand? It is one thing to make connections out of chaos, to fabricate unified landscapes, to create surface worlds in which the shortcomings of nature and the destructiveness of humans have been flushed out. (Some would say that this is precisely what art is for.) But the evidence of the works in this tradition – finished, immutable, fixed in their frames – is unequivocal. They are monuments to a relationship in which the artist is in absolute control of nature. However artistically satisfying they may be on their own terms they do not even address ecology's central ethical conundrum – how we may reconcile our special, distinguishing abilities as a uniquely creative kind of animal with our membership of the planetary community; how to be simultaneously the self-conscious artist and the aggregated amoeba.

Lewis Thomas has explored the ramifications of this paradox as eloquently as anyone, and in his celebrated essay 'Natural Man' he has described how we have been through at least two revolutions in thought about our relationship to nature. The oldest and most comfortable idea was that the earth was man's personal property, to be ordered, tamed, consumed as we wished. Then came the Ecological Enlightenment when there was a recognition that we were part of the system, as dependent on the health of the rest as trees or tadpoles. Now, whilst still believing in this new wisdom, we have come back to the realisation that, like it or not, we are in charge. He could very well be writing about the history of art in the late modern period:

> The truth is we have become more deeply involved than we
> ever dreamed. The fact that we sit around as we do, worrying
> seriously about how best to preserve the life of the earth, is
> itself the sharpest measure of our involvement. It is not human
> arrogance that has taken us in this direction, but the most natural
> of natural events. We developed this way, we grew this way, we
> are this kind of species . . . Perhaps, in the best of all possible
> worlds, functioning as a kind of nervous system for the whole
> being.

But this existential balancing act is one that we haven't mastered yet, and the reluctance of artists to grapple with it is a reflection of its difficulty. Only the group that, for want of a better label, are called 'land-artists' – Richard Long, Michael Fairfax, Andy Goldsworthy, David Nash, John Maine, et al – who are working directly with living materials, often *in situ*, seem to be exploring different energy flows and power structures in the relationship between humans and nature, which is echoed in that between artist and subject.

Land-art's long and eclectic range of influences lie in craftsmanship and writing as much as in the fine arts. In landscape painting a movement towards less anthropocentric work was characterised by closer and more equitable engagements with the subject. First the move down from the elevated – literally superior – viewpoint of the classic Claudian prospect; then an increasing emphasis on dense, detailed foregrounds as against formal but vague distances. Some of John Sell Cotman's Yorkshire watercolours (1805–7) in which the larger, *knowing* view is wilfully obstructed by teeming foreground vegetation are as far along this line of development as it was possible to go without abandoning the frame of the picture altogether.

The writing of the Romantics forms another important strand, exploring as it does the idea that humans may experience *themselves* as nature, as object as well as subject. Thomas Gray's account from the 1760s of a visit to Gordale Scar at Malham, in which he shudders for 'a full quarter of an hour' under the waterfall and the 'loose stones . . . which hang in the air, and threaten visibly', was an early, if gushing, example of the change in sensibility.

This sense that the observer can himself be the canvas was taken much further by Coleridge half a century later. His account of becoming stuck on a ledge during a hair-raising climb up Eskdale in 1802 is a crucial text:

> My limbs were all in a tremble – I lay upon my Back to rest myself, & was beginning according to my Custom to laugh at myself for a Madman, when the sight of the Crags above me on each side, & the impetuous Clouds just over them, posting

so luridly & so rapidly northward, overawed me / I lay in a state of almost prophetic Trance and Delight – & blessed God aloud, for the powers of Reason & the Will . . . I arose, and looking down saw at the bottom a heap of stones, which had fallen abroad and rendered the narrow ledge on which they had been piled doubly dangerous. At the bottom of the third Rock that I dropt from, I met a dead Sheep quite rotten. This heap of stones, I guessed, and have since found I guessed right, had been piled up by the Shepherd to enable him to climb up and free the poor Creature whom he observed to be crag-fast, but seeing nothing but rock over rock, he had desisted and gone for help and in the mean time the poor Creature had fallen down and killed itself. As I was looking at these I glanced my eye to the left, and observed that the Rock was rent from top to bottom. I measured the breadth of the Rent, and found that there was no danger of being *wedged* in, so I put my knap-sack round to my side, and slipped down as between two walls without any danger or difficulty . . . So I began to descend, when I felt an odd sensation across my whole breast . . . and on looking saw the whole of my Breast from my Neck to my Navel, exactly all that my Kamell-hair Breast-shield covers, filled with great red heat-bumps, so thick that no hair could lie between them . . . startling proof to me of the violent exertions I had made.

There are foretastes of all kinds of later preoccupations here: signs and portents in the landscape, the journey as an emotional record (the letter could easily be hung as *A Vertical Walk in the Lakes*), nature acting apparently benignly towards humans. Later that year Coleridge wrote that 'Everything has a Life of its own . . . we are all *one Life*.'

Another root is in the craftsmen who carved the decorative, naturalistic foliage that adorns many Gothic cathedrals. In their delight in ornamentation, in taking natural forms (the fingered leaf is, significantly, their favourite motif) and making them proliferate, join, evolve, play, mutate, they reached a harmonious marriage between human and natural invention. Perhaps the one misunderstanding Ruskin and Peter Fuller made in their love of Gothic was seeing only its austere, reverential aspect, the product of spiritual devotion and hard work. Yet Gothic is also satirical, impish, exuberant. And to this extent it more truthfully reflects the natural processes which inspired it.

It is dangerous to take analogies and value judgements too literally when talking about the natural world. But there is no doubt that for every aspect of natural creation that is brusquely functional there are others that are capricious, prolific and almost whimsical. The idea that nature is frugal and sternly purposeful, abhorring waste and pointlessness, is a product more of puritanism and the work ethic than of biology. More often it is profligate and experimental. The point about natural selection is not that it picks the high-fliers, the most perfectly adapted, the winners, but simply that it excludes the unworkable.

As a result (and accepting the absence of intention) the objective business of natural evolution is barely distinguishable from the business of artistic decoration. They are both part of that instinctive creativity that goes with being a living creature, Dylan Thomas's 'force that through the green fuse drives the flower'; both inventive explorations of matter and possibility, not of meaning. Function and concept follow, they do not precede natural creativity. Leaves fray at the edge, split into pairs, join up, multiply, change colour, drop off. Feathers are washed with iridescence and tonal change beyond any useful purpose. Feet grow supports, spikes and joints, with all the abandon of an animated cartoon. But it may only be much later that these accoutrements come in useful for gripping branches, balancing upright on the ground, running, kicking. And provided they don't actually disadvantage an organism their inventions persist, as pure embellishment. This kind of extravagant diversity is, in the global scale of things, nature's great defence against extinction, 'the dying of the light'. To that extent artistic ornamentation for its own sake has the highest sanction from nature and, perhaps, something of the sacramental about it.

Land-artists may feel that their inspiration comes chiefly from the Romantics, but the way they work seems to me to belong to the Gothic tradition. Like the Gothics they are celebrating natural forms more than human feelings. And much of their work follows a standard pattern, beginning with a natural object, adding 'human quickening' and then allowing nature to decide the final form or fate of the work. What evolves is neither strictly man-made nor natural, but is again a hybrid, an exploration of that crucial hinterland between two types of creativity. I like the modest and witty role they implicitly suggest for humans in nature, as inquisitive bowerbirds, leaving spoors, clues, puns and trophies to slowly find their way back into the earth.

Andy Goldsworthy is the most accessible and prolific of this group. Much of his work is a challenge to the idea of the immutable art object, and celebrates transience, natural weathering and decay, and the slow dissolution of one form into another. Even whilst they are still intact, his ice bridges and monumental sand castles are mercurial, changing with every declension of light and weather. Other works explore the qualities and potentialities of plants, probing their boundaries in time and space. A snowball, kept until mid-summer, melts to disgorge a winter's cargo of fir cones, daffodils, stones and debris. Chestnut and plane leaves are sewn together by pine needles or thorns, into the forms of boxes, horns, pyramids. They have a bewildering lightness and resilience that seems beyond the qualities of either leaves or boxes. They are *evolved* forms. Andy Goldsworthy's relationship with his material is like that of a rogue twist of DNA or a benign virus with its host cell. He worms his way into a bunch of twigs or a leaf, and sparks off new developments and mutations, new possibilities. And these may be political and social possibilities. His figure-of-eight sheepfold in his own patch of land is described as 'an exercise in sharing'. The entrance to his part of the fold lies in his neighbour's land, and his neighbour's in Andy's land. He is as much a messenger as creator, responding to moments and social moods, picking up stories in the wind and adding his distinctive style of invention.

Richard Long, by contrast, brings almost nothing of himself to his works:

> [It] is simple and practical . . . I like the idea of using the
> land without possessing it . . . My work has become a simple
> metaphor of life. A figure walking down his road, making his

mark. It is an affirmation of my human scale and senses: how far
I walk, what stones I pick up, my particular experiences. Nature
has more common means: walking, placing, stones, sticks, water,
circles, lines, days, nights, roads.

This sounds ecologically impeccable, a prescription for an art
that 'treads lightly on the earth', and it has produced some
poignant works, especially the ephemeral 'water drawings'. Yet I
wonder if it has any place in a gallery. What Long describes is the
commonplace, vernacular art of the outdoors, the universal habit of
arranging twigs, skimming stones, recounting journeys in the pub
at the end of the day. To elevate and frame this as fine art-work
is to make a very unecological appropriation of common cultural
property. If it was writing (which it very often is) it would be seen
as nothing more than rough notes.

Ironically, Long's insistence on minimal intervention also
undervalues *human* creativity – the quality that both Coleridge ('I
blessed God . . . for the powers of Reason & the Will') and Lewis
Thomas recognise as essential for any harmonious resolution of our
clouded relationships with nature.

David Nash has perhaps made the most successful marriage
between a powerful artistic vision and a respect for the independent life of nature. He works almost exclusively in wood, which he
sees as 'a weaving of earth and light', and says that 'the objects I
make are vessels for the presence of the human being, aware and
surrendering to the realities of nature'. The results are muscular
explorations of the nature of wood and the way it warps, cracks
and weathers that at times almost transcends its inherent woodiness. His elephant's trunk *Ubus* (titled after playwright Jarry's
caricatures of royalty) are even able to joke at the occasional
inelegance of tree growth. *Ash Dome* incorporates still-growing
material (a hemisphere of trained ash saplings) into the work.
Comet Ball is a large, aboriginal, almost comic-book cone, with
the rough-carved head charred in a bonfire, and is such a stunning,
elemental image that you feel it has come from a time when the
natural world – wood, fire and fantasy – was all of a piece. And
like the exhilarating series of *Running Tables* it comes close to that

ancient, benevolent myth – a symbol of a cooperative evolution and of the artistic process – the mixed life-form, the hybrid, the optimistic chimera.

1991

William Tillyer

Not many miles from William Tillyer's North Yorkshire retreat, Alfred Wainwright, England's favourite topographical artist, once set down an extraordinary account of an underground landscape. His sketch of Lancaster Hole is nothing special; a scatter of boulders round a pot-hole mouth in his familiar dot-matrix style. But his description of its discovery is like the beginnings of an aboriginal creation fable. A pot-holer had been resting up on the fells near Casterton. It was a day of dead calm, but he noticed a clump of grass quivering, as if it were being rustled by the wind. And, 'curiosity leading to investigation, he encountered a strong draught issuing from a small hole in the ground'. Eventually he found his way into a series of caverns, 'of immense halls with colonnades of massive stalagmites . . . of floors and shelves littered with cave pearls and crystals'. It turned out to be the oldest cave system in Britain, and this was the first time it had been touched by light. How does one begin to visualise this history, of astonishing ornamentation evolving in absolute darkness?

William Tillyer, whose new collection includes epic acrylic paintings as well as watercolours, has been working close to the rim of that mythic hole, peering like a dowser for the tell-tale shivers of the grass, and for the first signs and essentials of life to swim into the light. He refuses to accept that landscape painting must choose to be purely an exploration of nature or of space, colour and line, the painter's raw materials. At first light he can see little difference between the two.

The polarities that he is challenging are deeply embedded in our whole cultural attitude towards landscape. We persist in seeing it as surface, as object, as a kind of canvas itself. More damagingly (though understandably, given our need for some reassuring bulwark against change) we view it as fixed and finished, as 'heritage', when all the while it is still *becoming*, still 'issuing' from the earth.

Writing of Tillyer's watercolours Peter Fuller has suggested that 'in watercolours, and perhaps *only* in watercolours, the great cry of the romantic aesthetic (i.e. 'Truth to Nature') and that of emergent Modernism (i.e. 'Truth to Materials') were, in effect, one and the same'. Tillyer's exploitation of the fluid, *indefinite* qualities of watercolour does come close to catching the vitality and spontaneity of natural forms – and of those moments when we forget the mythology of 'timelessness' and glimpse the currents of growth and vulnerability that join us with the landscape.

In Tillyer's series of English Landscape Watercolours, 1985–87, it is possible to see even closer connections. So attentive are his explorations of the properties of water and colour that he can make quite specific topographical references without sacrificing any painterly qualities. In *Arnecliff, distant trees*, sap and water merge, and the rounded clumps of greenery seem like reflections of the sky. In *The Downs, outside Marlborough*, the jumbled swell of the chalk is a thickening echo of the tumulus formation above; as in geological history, the ground is formed out of the settling of myriads of water creatures.

This search for experiences and forms which are common both to nature and the Promethean business of painting continues in Tillyer's new collection of watercolours. The cellular shapes and primal colours recur: the curved washes of the sky are shaped like the buds of unopened leaves; a sliver of sun suggests an ear of corn (as Richard Jefferies wrote, 'in the wheatfield . . . transubstantiation is a fact').

But there is an additional element, reminiscent of his *Theme and*

166

Variations on a bridge over the Esk near his home (1983). All the watercolours contain a figurative, branching tree. It is a universal natural form, found in river systems and skeletons and lines on the face, and also an ancient human symbol of life. Here it is seen in all moods and moments, cosseted by hedges, sunburnt, drenched by (one suspects) acid rain. Washes of age and new growth pass across it, geometric man-made structures and louring pitch-dark clouds hover nearby. More often than is comfortable the tree seems about to be literally blotted out. In the acrylic paintings this troubled note becomes much sharper, giving almost a sense of petrification. Gone is the delicacy and tentativeness of the watercolours. The paint sweeps in hard, furious arcs across the canvas, curving and colliding. Some of Tillyer's familiar motifs and shapes can be glimpsed, but they are plastic and urgent, and reminiscent at times of Peter Lanyon.

But if Lanyon observed the world from up high, in a glider, Tillyer's acrylics have the eerie feeling of being landscapes painted from *beneath* the ground. They have an ancient, antediluvian air about them that perhaps derives from his experiences in southern Australia. The painter himself is apt to say that his colours are 'purely referential' – blue for sky, green for growth – but here those colours remind you more of jade and fluorspar. And if the watercolours suggest the gentle evolution of Cretacean England, formed under water and slowly shaped by it, the acrylics belong to an older, fiercer geological time, of magma and metamorphic rock. They are embryos rather than reductions, full of the excitement of things yet to be formed. If paint could be extruded between plates of rock, this is how it might set.

Yet even with such an apparently remote (though not abstract) view of the world as we normally perceive it, Tillyer keeps firmly in touch with the *processes* of nature. He paints his big pieces quickly, using a broom for the larger sweeps of colour, and the fast-setting acrylic bristles with evidence of this energetic movement. Here and there you can glimpse a frayed tree-shape in the paint, and you realise it makes not the slightest difference whether it is a deliberate device or a piece of serendipitous ageing.

167

It is hard not to be reminded of Turner's tremendous sense of time and moment. In Yorkshire, Turner often worked underground, and in Weathercote Cave in 1808 the scene before him changed fast and dramatically, being half-full of floodwater one moment or lit up by rainbows in the spray. Often, when he was sketching furiously in his notebook, he was unable to see what he was putting down.

Tillyer's pictures don't share Turner's literalness, but they too have been deeply affected by the turbulence of the real Yorkshire landscape. Indeed it would be hard to imagine how anyone could make sense of them without recognising that they are both a response to and an incorporation of real natural change.

His new collection seems to me to make two important statements. First, his use of materials implicitly challenges the assumption that it is possible, let alone desirable, to paint without reference to the physical world. Second, it extends his earlier view of the oneness of human and natural landscapes to include the raw stuff of the earth itself. Natural life, rock, paint and painter are all indivisibly linked.

What is perhaps the most outstanding acrylic has, from a distance, the rough profile of a butterfly. Near-to it is a tumult of vivid lava, and your eye is drawn into a vortex of filaments and flagellae, up and out towards a circle of light, the mouth of the cave.

1989

Christo

What a caper to have a show based chiefly on 'Projects Not Realised'. The idea could catch on. There could be recitals of fugues that never got beyond their subjects; anthologies (I have a promisingly thick file myself) of authors' aborted synopses. But perhaps with Christo it really doesn't matter if the works are completed, since so much of their power lies at a purely conceptual level, in the sheer, grandiloquent impertinence of his ideas.

He started modestly enough, with simple 'Wrapped Objects' in 1958. It was when he had the vision of putting something as substantial as a whole building or a geological formation in wraps that he became a public figure, and grist to every kind of cultural theorist. His work was the apotheosis of consumerism or a satire on it; he was a Marxist, exploring the 'objectification' of the physical world, or maybe just a conjuror with rather large silk handkerchiefs.

One of the 'unrealised' projects is a good example of the ambivalence of his work, and of how it scarcely needs to be finished to make its point. In 1968 he had a scheme for packing the Allied Chemical Tower in Times Square. The scale model is a delicious dig at this austere cathedral of the science business, and bundles it roughly up in polythene and twine like a delivery from the garden centre. Some, though, may see it as a homage to the building, wrapped in a shroud; or a comment on the secret mysteries of chemical structure; or a sexually political statement

169

on the arrogance of capitalism's masculine spires. Christo's work is, in McLuhan's terms, decidedly 'soft'. The one incontestable element is a good deal of benign fun at other people's expense. Confronting a Christo is always like waking up in Gotham and finding City Hall cloaked in pink satin. Is it really the Riddler, or just the Joker?

But the works in progress are more problematic. Taking shape on a huge scale in the real world, their indiscriminateness and lack of decisive purpose can make them seem politically naive or even offensive. No one but a killjoy could object to the Umbrellas Project, in which, for three weeks in October [1991], 3,100 coloured parasols will sprout like cocktail decorations simultaneously in valleys in California and eastern Japan. But I'm relieved 'Wrapped Trees, Project for the Champs Elysées' never saw the light of day, even temporarily. The rows of muffled limes and planes have, in the sketches at least, a miserly, municipal look, like a bureaucrat's way of keeping bird droppings off the parked Citroëns.

Events in the real world quite properly effect the meanings of public art. Christo's scheme for wrapping the Reichstag – 'a physical encounter of two values of life and human existence' – was first mooted in 1972. The recent tumultuous events in Eastern Europe have given new significance to what the artist regards as an indomitable 'symbol of Democracy'. Even his proposed materials seem serendipitously to prophesy the raising of the Iron Curtain, and make one look forward to the fourteen days in September when the work will be in place: 'The shiny light-coloured fabric will enlarge the size of the structure, it will be almost thirty per cent more voluminous, the folds of the fabric will take the force and direction of the wind and will make the building strangely and constantly breathing.'

But history has been less kind to *The Mastaba of Abu Dhabi*. Since the Gulf War this plan for a giant pyramidal anthem to oil has come to seem in thoroughly bad taste. Constructions from barrels have been one of Christo's preoccupations, and back in 1962 they had another (in retrospect ironic) meaning, when he built an *Iron Curtain-Wall of Oil Barrels* to block the Rue Visconti in Paris. Currently he is stacking 390,500 oil barrels for the Abu Dhabi project: 'Nothing comparable has ever existed in any other country. Hundreds of bright colours, as enchanting as the Islamic mosaics, will give a constantly changing visual experience according to the time of the day and the quality of the light.' Its intention, he says, is to be 'the symbol of civilisation of oil throughout the world' – a vision which certainly puts Mrs Thatcher's rhapsodies over the 'great car economy' in their place.

What this kind of declamatory art needs, I reckon, is not fewer public associations but more. One of the best aspects of Christo's works is the huge degree of popular involvement in their actual construction. The Mayles brothers' ebullient documentaries have caught this well, especially the festive communal raising of the famous *Running Fence* in California – two million square feet of nylon stretching over twenty-four miles. These events put Christo in a long tradition of outdoor vernacular art that includes England's chalk-hill carvings – which were scraped out by vast armies of workers, and in an atmosphere probably rather similar.

But it is worth remembering that public participation didn't end there, and that locals went on tinkering and scouring for centuries. It now seems, for instance, that the famously vast penis of the Cerne Abbas Giant was once a more modest organ, and that it was joined up with his navel by nineteenth-century Dorset rowdies bent on scandalising the local clergy. Demystifying Abu Dhabi's 'symbol of civilisation of oil' would be a more perilous business, but in a fine and ancient tradition.

1991

Peter Fuller and Ruskin

In the 1870s, as he sank deeper into spiritual disillusion, John Ruskin became convinced that England was blanketed by a terrible storm-cloud. He recoiled from thunderstorms 'like railway luggage trains – the air one loathsome mass of sultry and foul fog like smoke', and wrote to his friend Charles Norton that 'this sense of the evil working of nature itself – my disgust at her barbarity – clumsiness – darkness – bitter mockery of herself – is the most desolating'.

Despite advancing madness, he may not have been hallucinating. The North Country furnaces were already laying a pall of smog across the Lake District. But Peter Fuller believes that neither scientific nor psychological explanations are sufficient, and sees Ruskin's ominous vision as an augury of modernism. Gone was the idea of art as 'a channel of grace'; in its place a bleak conduit that would lead eventually to the belief in salvation through scientific progress and to the barren narcissism of Gilbert and George – an art whose only saving grace is that it accurately mirrors the age of Thatcher and Chernobyl.

Theoria is a painstaking (and, at times, pained) account of Ruskin's fall from radiant belief to something close to nihilism, as he wrestled with the nineteenth century's growing tensions between faith, art and nature. Fuller argues that Ruskin's crisis provides 'clues not only to the spiritual and aesthetic dilemmas of his time, but of our own', and he describes a personal loss of conviction which is almost a mirror image of Ruskin's: the slow collapse of the optimism of the 1960s, which was going to sweep away the old constrictions of metaphysics, and the awkward growth of a belief that the aesthetic response needs to be rooted in moral and spiritual values if it – and the world – is to survive.

Ruskin used the word *theoria* to describe 'the response to beauty of one's whole moral being'. He contrasted it with *aesthesis*, 'the mere sensual perception of the outward qualities and necessary effects of bodies', or 'the mere animal consciousness of the pleasantness' to which such effects gave rise. He was convinced that this distinction was a fundamental one in human perception, and that the physical discoveries of nineteenth-century science were eroding our sense of the 'true nature' of the world. In his late teens he had looked more favourably on science, which he had hoped would reveal the divine hand behind creation. But the revelations of natural theology began increasingly to trouble him. Plants had sex lives (which Ruskin hardly did). Species came and went. William Buckland's work on early fossils was leading to the heretical and disturbing notion that there might have been death *before* the Fall. Worst of all was the tendency of natural theology to attribute all design in nature to function. Ruskin argued that this kind of practical understanding could seriously inhibit an imaginative response to beauty, and that if we are told that the leaves of a plant are 'occupied in decomposing carbonic acid, and preparing oxygen for us, we begin to look upon it with some indifference as a gasometer'.

But the exuberance of nature couldn't be pigeon-holed so tidily, and when the Pre-Raphaelites began to show their pictures in the 1850s Ruskin was already uncertain about his distinction between *theoria* and *aesthesis*. In his qualified defence of Charles Collins's 1851 picture, *Convent Thoughts*, he dismisses its laboured Tractarian symbolism, the starched nun contemplating a passion flower in her walled garden. Instead, he lavishes praise on the tangle of pondweeds at her feet. Never had he seen water plantain, *Alisma plantago*, 'so thoroughly or so well drawn'. It was a deliberate piece of contrariness, which suggested that deep-rooted detail was 'truer' than arcane but superficial symbol. The irony – dismissed a little too casually by Fuller – is that Ruskin misidentified the plant. It was not *Alisma*, a plant that he had picked out as a model of Gothic proportions and whose mathematically perfect leaf curvatures suggested to him the infinity of God, but arrowhead, *Sagittaria sagittifolia*.

This bizarre botanical rune-casting, and its even more curious failure, may give a clue to Ruskin's forced distinction between *theoria* and *aesthesis*, and his depression during the passage of 'the Storm Cloud of the Nineteenth Century'. Just when he might have found most solace in nature, he unaccountably turned against it. As Fuller puts it, he had come to fear that 'spirit having no nature, nature might have no spirit'.

Fuller takes Ruskin's earlier veneration of nature at face value, but there is evidence that it masked a more conventional and less creditable attitude. In 1855 he visited Ford Madox Brown, and examined his painting *An English Autumn Afternoon*. It is a splendid, effervescent picture, full of life and movement, with two animated lovers almost in the same plane as the vast ornamental panorama of Hampstead's trees, and, you might think, a perfect illustration of Ruskin's political and aesthetic ideas. But he called it a 'very ugly subject', a response that becomes more comprehensible when it is considered alongside his paternalistic social theories, and his belief in the hierarchies of the Great Chain of Being. The fact is that *theoria* was less a response guided by nature than a system imposed on it, and it was when nature refused to play by the elegant but suffocating rules decreed by Ruskin that he began to disown it. No wonder that the predominant types of nature in his work are passive or inanimate, the fossil in the rock and the plucked leaf; that he was obsessed with form ('Art [is concerned] only with appearances'), yet showed almost no interest in natural processes or relationships; that his models of human communities were the assemblies of leaves on trees.

In this he is firmly in the tradition of a vision of nature which revolves around Man, as God's estate manager. His old mentor, William Buckland, had once proclaimed that the rich mineral deposits of Britain expressed 'the most clear design of Providence to make the inhabitants . . . the most powerful and the richest nation on earth'. And this image of the world as a garden made specifically for the human race persists up to the present day. Even a radical phenomenologist such as Gregory Bateson, quoted approvingly by Fuller, can say that 'there is at least an impulse still in the human breast to unify and thereby to sanctify the total natural world of which we are' – as if it were *not* unified without the presence and blessing of humans.

The in-fightings and schisms which characterised nineteenth-century philosophy occupy a good deal of space in Peter Fuller's book, and it is easy to lose track of the broad lines of thought with which Ruskin was involved. Unquestionably, though, one of his major legacies was to explore the relations between nature and the Gothic style. His own preoccupation was partly a political one, and Fuller describes how he 'saw in the variety and idiosyncrasies of Gothic architecture a guarantee of the life and labour of every workman who struck the stone'. Yet there are suggestions that he saw the fact of ornament, of 'grace' in the musical sense, as a feature of all living things. Ruskin's hostility to any whiff of functionalism was too deep-rooted for him to go one stage further and glimpse that ornament and excess and intricacy are what gives nature its resilience, as well as its beauty. The shapes of leaves, the elaboration of bird-song, the diversity of species, the whole of what Annie Dillard has called 'the free, fringed tangle' of the world, are almost entirely pointless and unnecessary – except that they provide a hardiness and exuberance that is a bulwark against extinction and the creeping chill of entropy.

The idea of nature as random luxuriance does not square comfortably with *theoria*, especially as many of the consequences (large sweat glands finding a use as proto-nipples, for instance) teeter over into surrealism. But Peter Fuller, in his fine closing chapters, traces the thin threads which join Ruskin's ideas to those of modern biology. On the way he finds some unexpected allies: the aesthete Walter Pater, and his search for an 'equivalent for the sense of freedom' compatible with scientific understanding;

and John Berger, seemingly retreating from at least part of his ideological stance in *Ways of Seeing*: 'The notion that art is a mirror of nature is one that appeals only in periods of scepticism. Art does not imitate nature, it imitates a creation, sometimes to propose an alternative world, sometimes to simplify, to confirm, to make social the brief hope offered by nature.'

Peter Fuller suggests that Ruskin might have concurred with this view, though it seems some way from the anthropocentrism that lurks beneath all his ideas. At times Fuller too seems under its sway. He rightly finds echoes of Ruskinism in E. O. Wilson's theory of 'biophilia' (the urge to affiliate with other forms of life); and in fractal mathematics, which charts the indefinable, frayed or 'fringed' geometry of living things. But the fullest modern expression of Gothic philosophy, James Lovelock's *Gaia*, is not mentioned. This relegates humans to a participatory rather than a dominant role in a self-regulating Creation. Its great virtue as a foundation for aesthetic theory is that it narrows the gap between *aesthesis* and *theoria*. In Gaia, sensual and sensory response *become* moral – otherwise the whole system falls apart. The biologist Lewis Thomas once imagined the whole biosphere singing to itself, making music at the same time as keeping in tune: 'global hormones, keeping balance and symmetry in the operation of various interrelated working parts, informing tissues in the vegetation of the Alps about the state of the eels in the Sargasso Sea, by long interminable relays of interconnected messages between all kinds of other creatures'.

1988

James Lovelock and Gaia

Halfway along the overgrown road that links James Lovelock's Devon mill-house with the outside world is a meticulously printed sign with the message 'Experimental Station. Please Shut the Gate'. There is something beguiling about this mixture of rustic civility and slight scientific menace, lapped by ferns and standing in the middle of nowhere. But it is an apt entrance to the world of a man who is something of a paradox himself: one-time NASA advisor and champion of 'small science'; visiting Professor of Cybernetics at Reading University and enthusiast for nineteenth-century farming. And now internationally known as the originator of a unifying theory of global ecology which welds a commitment to scientific advance to a belief that nature knows best: the Gaia hypothesis.

Lovelock has been an independent and maverick scientist ever since the post-war years, when he would piece together his apparatus from war-surplus gear bought in Soho. It was an invention to measure minute concentrations of gases that led to his theory, which states that the geology, atmosphere and living systems of the Earth are linked in a self-regulating system, called Gaia after the Greek name for the Earth goddess. The system is coherent enough, Lovelock believes, for the living skin of the planet to be regarded as a super-organism in its own right. The theory goes beyond conventional ecology in suggesting that the living systems of the planet, far from being at the mercy of, say, climate and geological process, collectively manipulate their environment to keep conditions supportive of life. Gaia will (automatically and unconsciously, of course) put this objective above the survival of any individual species – humans included.

Since it was launched in 1977 (in *Gaia: A New Look at Life on Earth*) the theory has risen to the status of a myth. For many readers it has underlined the interconnectedness of life, validated holism, put man in his place. New Age pagans, normally contemptuous of science, have taken it as 'proof' of the existence of an Earth goddess. More rationally minded Greens have found it sketching in some of the long chains of cause and effect through which human activities influence the planet.

But the theory has attracted notoriety, too. The left (suspicious of Lovelock anyway for his attacks on the politicisation of ecology) deplore the theory as fatalistic and anti-human; while conventional science has accused it of being experimentally unfounded and verging on the mystical. Perhaps it is no wonder that its inventor (or, as he prefers to describe himself, rediscoverer) has retreated to this secluded valley, a mile from the nearest house, and cut off from all telephone communications except the fax machine.

Lovelock is far from being a recluse, though. He lives here with his second wife Sandy and son John, a colony of peacocks and a battery of computers, and does *not* grow organic vegetables. He has a small laboratory in the house and, with some industrial support, continues to refine his analysing equipment. One of the old barns houses a sophisticated dilution chamber, in which he can work on precisely measured low concentrations of gases like CFCs. 'It wouldn't work in a city or university lab,' he explains. 'One person with an aerosol deodorant at the end of the corridor could throw the measurement.'

We are talking in the summer, at the end of what has been a hectic month for Lovelock. He has just been honoured by the Dutch Academy of Science, and featured in Channel Four's *Visionaries* series. In a couple of weeks' time he is to be the local guest in a West Country edition of *Any Questions*. What he hasn't seen is the contents of a virulent, full-page attack on him in the *Guardian* by an Oxford ecologist, which rails against the growing 'irrationalism and dogma of . . . Popular Ecology', and points the finger at Lovelock as 'pre-eminent amongst the causes of this shift', which will eventually lead to the arrival of 'the Thought Police'. He reads my copy with increasing amusement, and it is obvious that he relishes being a stirrer of hornets' nests. As we talk it also becomes clear that the precepts of the Gaia theory and the views Lovelock has of the procedures and profession of science are intimately connected. The mill-house is neither an ark nor a hermit's cell, but it does reflect some of the principles of intimacy and localness that he sees operating in Gaia.

'I've always thought that science was something to be done at home, like writing or painting, a kind of cottage industry if you like.' When he delivered the Schumacher Lecture in 1988 he made this point even more explicitly: 'I take the advice to think globally by acting locally most seriously. I practise global science as a family business . . . not as some vast, remote and potentially dangerous activity.' There is something almost wilful in his determination to stay clear of institutional pigeon-holes, and though he is one of the Greens' heroes he repeatedly upbraids them when they take up 'inappropriate' issues, or mount arguments based on flawed evidence or 'political' preconceptions. He is sanguine about nuclear energy ('an entirely natural process') and the burning of PCBs ('no one makes them any more and they need to be destroyed'). Indeed there aren't many examples of what is conventionally regarded as pollution that he considers to be ecologically important – but not because he underestimates the threat they pose to the quality of human lives. He repeatedly makes the distinction between the degradation of human social life and damage to the biosphere, what he describes as 'people problems' and 'planet problems'. They don't always coincide, and wishful holistic thinking to the contrary is just another example of the difficulty we have in seeing things in other than human-centred ways.

The death of Aral Sea in Russia, for example, probably has little global significance. But Lovelock acknowledges that the destruction of the environment of thirty million Central Asians by a mixture of bureaucratic folly and ignorant agriculture is a human tragedy without precedent. He is constantly bemused by the fact that a nation which occupies a fifth of the world's land space is not even able to feed its own people. Nor does he see much hope for improvement in the short term. 'The sums the Russians are asking for in aid from the West are chicken-feed. They will not even begin to solve their problems.'

The issue that he puts at the top of the list is clearance of the tropical rain-forests for agriculture – though not for the usual reasons of loss of potentially useful plant species and rare animals (a typical 'people problem', ironically).

'The tropical climate is ideal for trees, but this isn't a given state of the Earth. The conditions are maintained by the trees themselves.' The rain-forest is a microcosm of Gaia. The trees keep their climate just the way they like it by the shade of their canopies and by the evaporation of vast volumes of water through their leaves. This water vapour forms a cloud cover which eventually falls back on the trees. The trees and rain form a single system; there can't be one without the other. If the trees are cleared, the rain they produce ceases, the cloud cover disappears, and in the direct heat of the sun the ground can rapidly turn to desert.

'There is still enough rain-forest for its cloud cover to have a considerable effect on global climate, especially in reflecting sunlight back to space. Every acre that is cleared adds a tiny increment to the earth's warming.

'I've recently had a go at costing out what the rain-forests are worth in terms of their cooling effect. You can do this by estimating what it would cost to refrigerate the same area artificially. The forest cloud cover reduces the heat reaching the canopy by about ten per cent. To get the same cooling effect you would need a refrigerator with a power of eighty-four kilowatts per acre, which would cost about £30,000 per annum. After they have been cleared for cattle the yield rarely gets above £100 an acre. These figures mean that the climatic value of the remaining forest in Amazonia alone is £450 trillion.'

Typically, Lovelock adds an example of the wrong way of looking at the problem: 'The Brazilians had a go at costing their forests, too, but they made the mistake of trying to value them as the major producers and exporters of oxygen. It was an interesting idea, but the net output of oxygen in a forest is almost zero. The local animals and micro-organisms use up most of it themselves.'

The transactions between the atmosphere and the various inhabitants of the Earth have always fascinated Lovelock. In the 1950s he perfected the electron capture detector, a refinement of the gas chromatograph which was able to detect substances at very low concentration. It is so sensitive that if a drum of a particular fluorocarbon was allowed to evaporate in Japan, the gas would be detectable in Britain a few days later. It was this instrument that enabled scientists in the 1960s to grasp the extent to which pesticides were persisting and spreading throughout the globe. It picked up DDT in Antarctic penguins, and Dieldrin in the milk of nursing mothers in Finland, and provided the data with which Rachel Carson was able to write *Silent Spring*, the book that turned into the first text of the burgeoning green movement.

In the 1960s NASA invited Lovelock to help devise ways of assessing whether there was life on Mars. His talent for lateral thinking led him to suggest what he calls 'a top-down view of the whole planet' instead of the more conventional idea of a search at the landing point. This would involve analysing the composition of the red planet's atmosphere. If Mars was lifeless, its atmosphere would be determined by physical and chemical processes alone, and would probably have reached some sort of chemical equilibrium. But if it carried life – at least in some quantity – then its organisms would almost certainly need to use the atmosphere as a source of food and energy, and a depository for waste matter, and these would register in its composition. The much-lived-in atmosphere on Earth could be used as a bench mark.

In the end it proved possible to do the measurements from Earth by infra-red astronomy. The results showed an astonishing divergence between the atmospheres of the two planets. The atmosphere of Mars was dominated by carbon dioxide, and was close to chemical equilibrium. By contrast the envelope of gases surrounding the Earth contained only traces of carbon dioxide, and was exceptionally unstable in composition. (Lovelock, fond of using cars as metaphors, likens Earth's atmosphere to the combustible mixture of gases entering a carburettor, and Mars's to those leaving the exhaust pipe.) The coexistence, over aeons of time, of stable concentrations of active gases like oxygen and methane was a chemical impossibility without some intervening agency to top up their levels. Oxygen in particular ought to have reacted with almost everything until it was virtually exhausted (levels on lifeless Mars are just 0.13 per cent). Instead levels have stayed constant at around 21 per cent for some hundreds of millions of years. A few per cent lower and complex life forms could not survive; a few per cent higher and all surface plant life would become dangerously combustible.

The average air temperature of the Earth has also remained surprisingly steady. Despite a 25 per cent increase in the amount of solar energy reaching us since life began three-and-a-half billion years ago, the mean atmospheric temperature has oscillated between the narrow limits of ten and twenty degrees Celsius. Again, a shift much beyond either of these limits would have meant the eventual elimination of life.

Lovelock became convinced that the long reign of these improbable and unstable circumstances could only have come about if the life-systems of the planet had evolved mechanisms for regulating their environmental conditions. And the more he looked into the chemistry of the Earth's skin, the more examples of this there seemed to be. There was, for instance, the puzzlingly low concentration of carbon dioxide in the air. Most scientists agree that as a result of volcanic eruption CO_2 levels were high at the start of life, and if the atmosphere was simply an inert sink there is no reason why it should have declined to its current status as a trace gas. But it was essential that this should have happened, because, even when it originates 'naturally', carbon dioxide acts as a greenhouse gas, preventing radiated and reflected heat from leaving the Earth, and high levels could have maintained temperatures too high for most life.

Although land-bound plants take up carbon dioxide, it is unlikely that they act as regulators, since they release the gas again as soon as they die and decay. But terrestrial plants and bacteria erode alkaline rocks so that these can chemically take up CO_2 more rapidly. There are also hosts of small organisms in the sea that, either directly or as elements in the food chain, use dissolved carbon dioxide to form calcium carbonate for shells and skeletons. As they die, their remains rain slowly down to the sea bottom to form submarine chalk and limestone, taking the carbon out of the cycle for very long periods. Since the numbers of these marine organisms increase with the raised temperatures associated with high CO_2 levels, they could form a natural thermostat.

The mechanisms that may be involved in these self-regulating cycles are remarkable, but far from mysterious. They can all be explained by conventional theories of natural selection. An organism which has evolved the ability to regulate its own environment has obviously improved its chances of survival over one that hasn't. Similarly, an organism which is able to improve the survival potential of those species it uses as food, or associates with, also has an edge.

If the kind of regulatory mechanisms that Lovelock proposes do exist, are they robust enough to withstand the stresses to which we are currently subjecting the planet? Could we, for instance, ever witness the evolution in estuaries of specialist bacteria which were able to remove polluting metals such as mercury and cadmium from the system, as well as carbon? The problem is that these kinds of mechanisms take many millions of years to evolve and may not be able to keep up with the pace of change at present. On balance Lovelock thinks that Gaia probably will be able to manage, but not necessarily in ways that will guarantee the survival of higher forms of life. Our ability to weather the storms to come depends, he believes, as much on our willingness to work *within* the rules of Gaia as on outright scientific cleverness.

For him this has meant a personal rather than a political response. The temperament that made him pursue his career as an independent scientist makes him look for small-scale solutions. 'If you take a Gaian view, things always start off from the action of an individual organism, an individual gene. It doesn't have to be a very big change to make a big difference in the long-term.'

Lovelock's own initiative was the move to Devon, and the gradual purchase of more than thirty acres of rough farmland around the mill. With the help of grants he has planted this up with 20,000 trees, and is leaving much of the rest to go wild. We walk round it, and, with buzzards wheeling overhead and the overgrown hedges ringing with warblers' song, it is like a vision of the bittersweet days of Victorian farming. He has an ambivalent attitude towards farming, respecting the contract with the land that traditional practices represented, but regarding modern agrobusiness (and cattle rearing especially) as one of the worst blights on the earth. He points angrily to some fields on a neighbouring farm, stripped recently of their hedges, and already drying out so much that the few remaining trees are showing their roots.

He hopes his own trees will serve a double purpose. Trees 'buy time', tying up carbon dioxide for a few centuries at least. He also sees them restoring some of the 'natural seemliness, free from any taint of the city' that he remembers from the countryside of his boyhood. I ask if he will harvest them for fuel, but he has no great enthusiasm for wood-burning stoves, and prefers what he regards as the more efficient and cleaner power supply of the national grid. He parades very few of the tokens and paraphernalia that are usually associated with ecologically minded households. There are no solar panels and no private recycling arrangements. The public are not allowed to walk even on the outskirts of his property. Lovelock sees more value in his preserving a small stretch of wild land than in gestures which are essentially designed to make human life more tolerable.

Nor will he be drawn into suggesting neat panaceas for global ecological crises while our understanding of how the planet works under normal conditions is so poor. When his stint on *Any Questions* came up, the home audience was audibly disappointed by his restrained response ('cut down on cars and plant trees') to a wide-ranging question about 'what we could do', and for his support for Mrs Thatcher's environmental platform (to which he gives marks for conservatism as much as Toryism, I suspect).

His distaste for environmental politicking may seem disingenuous in the light of this. But it is consistent with his philosophy, and with a favourite aphorism: 'There are no prescriptions in Gaia; only consequences.' To the extent that he has a policy for the future it is to wait, watch and think. When the crisis arrives – and he believes it is inevitable – what we should do will be much clearer. He likens our position now to that of Britain in 1936. 'People knew that a war was coming. They chatted about what they would do. But it wasn't until it started that they began to take sensible measures to cope.' Inside the cautious scientist there is something of an old-style Roundhead, an English Revolutionary (an echo of a youth spent as an agnostic Quaker perhaps) who thinks that a good crisis might do a lot to concentrate our minds. In his address to the 1989 conference of Friends of the Earth he said: 'I believe that soon the prospect of large and daunting changes will be seen. Then we shall become aware of a larger need and science will cease its pettifogging and come together as it did under the lesser stress of war. It might even evolve to become like the science of 1940, a shining vocation, lean and fit and tough in mind and heart.' That is about as close as he will go to giving comfort to an increasingly anxious humanity. The disturbances that will be precipitated by global warming will be surprising and probably nasty. There will be turbulent weather and unpredictable social and political consequences. He thinks that, to give the greener parts of the earth time to adapt and recover, humans should withdraw as much as possible to the cities (though he still believes that 'city life reinforces the heresy of humanism, that narcissistic devotion to human interests alone').

He is far from fatalistic, though. He thinks we should try as much as we can – within our present knowledge – to press more lightly on Gaia's mechanisms, but not presume to put them into intensive care. He gives many examples of well-meaning but ill-thought-out 'solutions' whose consequences have been decidedly double-edged. Biodegradable plastic, for instance, which seems irreproachably Green, but whose increasing popularity will rob us of one of the more effective means of tying up lethal carbon dioxide: the *non*-biodegradable plastic. Or the tragedy that befell Lapland in the wake of the Chernobyl nuclear disaster, about which he has written: 'thousands of reindeer, the food prey of the Lapps, were destroyed because it was thought they were too radioactive to eat. Was it justifiable to inflict this brutal treatment for mild radio-active poisoning on a fragile culture and its dependent ecosystem?' Lovelock is on the reindeers' side, and more particularly on the side of the Earth's bacteria and micro-organisms and lower plants, for whom he has nominated himself 'shop steward'. It is these that make the world go round and make up the heart of Gaia, not the essentially free-loading higher animals. And it is in their heartlands – in the soil and rain-forests and continental shelves especially – where the fate of planetary ecology may be decided.

If the left dislike his view of the human species as 'just one member of a very democratic planetary community', many middle-of-the-road biologists abhor his disregard for the niceties of scientific etiquette. Prominent amongst his critics are what he styles 'the Oxford neo-Darwinists' centred around Richard Dawkins. Love-lock calls himself a classical Darwinist, but still admires Dawkins' celebrated 'selfish gene' theory, and his initiative in modelling evolutionary pathways on a computer. He cannot understand the sheer vitriol of the attacks that come from some Dawkinsians (such as Dr John Horsfall's *Guardian* piece). He is perplexed by their charges that the Gaia hypothesis is unscientific because it cannot be falsified, and that it presupposes that altruism can exist in non-thinking systems.

But neo-Darwinists of all people ought to have a care before accusing others of creating untestable hypotheses. The whole framework of evolutionary theory is untestable, since it refers to particular, unrepeatable events in the past. No one can ever check out the mechanism of the evolution of red blood cells, let alone of a whole order such as the dinosaurs. The theory of evolution stands (as the Gaia hypothesis will stand or fall eventually) on a considerable weight of circumstantial evidence, not rigorous scientific proof.

Nor is it right to suggest that Gaia assumes the existence of 'altruism' in lower orders of life. In Lovelock's view its mechanisms are all entirely automatic, worked out over aeons of trial and error and mutual adjustment. Each new species on the Earth evolved not on a *tabula rasa* but in the atmospheric and environmental conditions set by its predecessors; we breathe in the air that plants 'breathe' out. Each increase in biological diversity extends the resilience and flexibility of the system in response to change. Collectively the system cannot *but* be interactive.

Gaia could be seen as the solution to an immense number of simultaneous equations, each one of which describes the relationship of a given species with its environment. Or, as Lovelock's close colleague Lynn Margulis has put it: 'Each species to a greater or lesser degree modifies its environment to optimise its reproduction rate. Gaia follows from this by being the sum total of all these individual modifications and by the fact that all species are connected, for the production of gases, food and waste removal, however circuitously, to all others.'

I ask Lovelock whether he ever wishes he had opted for a low-profile definition like this rather than going on to describe the Earth as an organism in its own right. He retorts that even conventional biologists are now prepared to use the phrase 'super-organism' about complexes like beehives and termite mounds. So why not about the Earth? But he admits that, yes, he was being deliberately provocative. 'I wanted to stir them into thinking about the whole planet.' He is coming round to the view that it doesn't matter whether the full Gaian theory is true or not, provided that we learn to take a 'top-down view of the Earth' and to think in terms of 'planetary physiology'.

My own view is that the theory may turn out to be a kind

of high-level tautology, that the biosphere simply could not exist in any other way. We now regard as self-evident, for instance, the notion that all animals are perfectly constructed for what they are and where they live, although this was an heretical idea in the human-centred view of the eighteenth century.

Or perhaps Gaia is not so much a single organism as a tightly-knit group, rather like a remarkable species of weevil recently discovered in New Guinea. *Symbiopholus* lives with dozens of plants growing in the crack in its shell and rooted in its flesh, and is 'gardened' by a whole ecosystem of insects and bacteria. It is 3 centimetres in length, and lives a long life, untroubled by predators.

Either way I suspect that it will be Gaia's power as a metaphor that turns out to be its enduring feature (though this may please neither Lovelock nor his critics). Although Lovelock is right to emphasise that individual organisms are important in Gaia, what shines out most strongly from the theory is the idea of mutuality, of the interdependence of all organisms and their environments. Humans, quite properly, will always want to play their part in this, to help out, to have their place in the sun (and in the countryside), to use their unique biological gifts of intelligence and creativity.

James and I are both admirers of the American biologist and writer Lewis Thomas, and I remind him of the passage in Thomas's *Lives of a Cell* (1974) where he describes a future for the human species as 'handyman to the earth' ('I would much prefer this useful role ... to the essentially unearthly creature we seem otherwise on the way to becoming'). Lovelock smiles, gives the phrase the slightest twist and says, 'Employed *by* the Earth. Yes, I like that!' He is already beginning to take a more benevolent view of an actively engaged humanity himself. He has always recognised that the Gaia can survive without humans, but not vice versa, and is currently working on a new book, a 'textbook of planetary medicine' – what we might be able to do, without making things worse, to help alleviate acid rain, famines, global warming, etc. Despite his hostility towards 'big science' it will discuss the contributions which might be made by private, corporate 'planetary physicians' (Shell's scheme for burning power-station coal in pure oxygen and liquefying the carbon dioxide, for instance. Or producing more purely synthetic food to take the pressure off the land).

But mostly it will be medicine of the barefoot, preventative and minimum intervention kind. Fundamentalist Gaians see humans at best as shamans – interpreting and conjuring nature but never really presuming to intervene in it. It will be fascinating to see how far Lovelock himself has moved towards viewing us as altogether more actively involved, and perhaps in the therapeutic role that he seems to fit most closely himself: the quirky, eclectic, not always consistent but resolutely wise Planetary GP.

1990

PART FOUR

Landmarks

A Sense of Occasion

"Jan 3: 1903. Am writing an essay on the life-history of insects and have abandoned the idea of writing on 'How Cats Spend their Time'." So W. N. P. Barbellion began his classic *Journal of a Disappointed Man*. He was only thirteen at the time, and I have heartfelt sympathy with his sense of not being quite in control of the rudder. After a year of public journal writing I am struck by how haphazard the whole business is. Too few facts, too many rushed judgements, a marked tendency to make extravagant flourishes of private emotions.

But fits of self-doubt are endemic to writers. I sometimes try to assuage mine by pretending that writing is a legitimate rural trade, and prose a kind of alternative crop, yielding so many bushels of word to acres tramped. If so, I can report that there is little danger of a surplus word mountain building up in this corner of the countryside. To tell the truth the whole business feels more like hunter-gathering than farming. There is the same element of serendipity, of lucky finds and blank days; the same merging of roles, so that foraging becomes part of everything you do.

Which is why, in a rare spell of balmy weather in February, I found myself walking down a familiar track in a mood in which it was impossible to disentangle childish excitement and professional curiosity. The evening before I had seen the glint of running water where no running water had been for a decade, and I was off, chasing whole volumes of memory and possibilities.

I have walked these hills to the south of my home since I was a teenager, and the route has become almost a ritual beat. It is an unexceptional landscape of run-down parkland and narrow commons. But after thirty years you can come to love every fencepost. And in this unseasonable weather there was a wild *frisson* in the air – a thin gauze of green already in the hedges, rooks tossing over the copses, and gale-wrecked trees in every field, already seeming as cryptic and anciently rooted as standing stones.

At the edge of Icedell Wood was the most awesome collapse I have seen following the hurricane [in October 1987]; eight oak trees on a single root-plate 15 feet high and nearly 40 feet across. The branches on the two central trees had grown away from each other, forming a huge vaulted aisle now they were prostrate. I walked up and down this immense whale's gullet, counting my steps. It was more than 130 feet long.

I wriggled through the tangled branches into the wood. Drifts of tits and chaffinches, fellow foragers, rose and fell in front of me. Under the beeches by the old icehouse, the first green hellebores were already in flower, only days behind the celandines, and on the same site they were recorded in our first county flora in 1848.

I know their history, I rejoice in their continuity, yet I barely glance at them. I realise I have been racing through the wood, drawn by the lure of water and driven by workaday anxieties that I haven't yet unwound from. Just a few hours before I had been listening to a radio reading of Henry Reed's famous war poem 'Naming of Parts', in which he contrasts the stripping down of a rifle with the first stirrings of a garden after winter:

> And this you can see is the bolt. The purpose of this
> Is to open the breech, as you see. We can slide it
> Rapidly backwards and forwards: we call this
> Easing the spring. And rapidly backwards and forwards
> The early bees are assaulting and fumbling the flowers:
>   They call it easing the Spring.

Just a few hundred yards more and I am in the valley, barely able to stop running. That distant glint of water had been no mirage. Our local winterbourne, the Woewater, is up and flowing for the first time in a dozen years. The vast winter rains are bursting through the seams between the clay and chalk and charging down the valley. Within half a mile the stream is four feet wide and flowing as fast as I can walk. It has torrents and oxbows and eddies, and underneath them the young meadow grass is waving as silkily as waterweed. In one dip it has formed a pool by the edge of a wood, and bubbles rising from buried air pockets look like summer midges settling on the surface. I am time-warped, and for a few seconds am seized by a conviction that the first swallow will coast down the valley and begin hawking over the pool.

It doesn't, of course, but a mile or so further on I see something almost as wondrous. The stream has flooded the valley meadows, and flocks of fieldfares and redwings are feeding near the water's edge. A snipe jinks in the distance and, much closer, a heron flies up from a pond that has been a dry pit since I was a teenager. The water suddenly makes sense of the whole geography of the valley – the position of the farms, the ancient black poplar, standing again with its roots in water.

There is a legend here that the Woewater only flows in times of war and trouble, but it is hard to see how it could have brought anything but good to this dry valley.

Back home I check my diary to see if I had recalled the last rising accurately. I noted it on 12 April 1975 – a year memorable more for its wonderful summer than any particular woe, and for the fact that the fighting in Vietnam ended a fortnight later. I am not superstitious, but think that might be a better kind of legend to hang on to. The rising of water, like sap, is another kind of easing the spring.

Later that month I paid a visit to east Suffolk – a very different landscape but another old stamping ground. Years ago I had a little retreat just inland from the heaths and marshland round the Blyth estuary, and always found the close weave of human and natural habitats oddly comforting. In summer nightingales sang in the churchyard and marsh harriers hunted down the field edges. In winter we used to sit in the bar of the Harbour Inn at Southwold and watch short-eared owls wheeling over the Town Marshes.

It can be risky returning to places where you have been happy in the past, and at first the omens weren't good. The marshland nature reserves along the coast looked marvellous, but were shorn of birds. But then they started to appear, between the seams and at the edge of things, in the unofficial landscapes. Grey wagtails looped along the roadside dykes and yellowhammers flocked in the stackyards. Half a mile from my old cottage a hen harrier was creating panic amongst a flock of pigeons, on exactly the same rough headland where I used to watch harriers fifteen years previously. That evening I went looking for barn owls in the Blyth flood meadows. I failed completely, but ought to have expected the one that was circling my car (parked by a roadside gorse patch) as I walked back.

The eighteenth-century essayist William Hazlitt, trying to explain the roots of the 'love of country' found it in our attachment to 'common and familiar images', and suggested that nature was 'a kind of universal home'. It isn't really surprising that humans and nature often head for the same kind of retreats, out on the margins, where the pattern of life hasn't yet been fixed. In these turbulent times it might do us no harm to resurrect the old idea of 'the nature sanctuary' – a place defined not by immutable boundaries and fixed species lists, but by the chances it offers for growth and refuge.

Fleeing to Holland's northern wetlands from a Britain buffeted by spring monsoons and a string of environmental crises was like journeying to one of those parallel universes beloved of science-fiction writers. The shrivelling weather was as bad (worse,

196

see, eg. MICHIO KAKU's (a leading physicist) book Parallel Worlds 2005 actually), the political climate just as unsettled. But in place of the mood of glum confrontation we had left behind, there was wit and inventiveness in the air.

The Dutch are masters of the political side-step, the social pun. And faced with a problem, they often seem able not just to think their way laterally out of it, but to make some kind of parable in the process. Is there another small country where the flower markets make up for the shortage of garden space by selling sprouting coconuts as house plants? Or one which edges country park lay-bys with stones painted in the form of miniature sleeping sheep?

We had gone chiefly to watch birds on the polders, those new marshlands won out of the Zuider Zee. Yet even in the heart of Amsterdam the Dutch knack of finding user-friendly solutions to environmental problems was apparent. We inadvertently fell foul of the parking laws one day, and were wheel-clamped by something resembling an outsize bulldog clip. This isn't the kind of penalty you can buy your way out of with a standing order from petty cash; and not at all like the Byzantine theatre of London clamping. In the city that gave the world the communal White Bicycle, what you must do is walk down one of the canal-sides to a post office, pay a nominal fine, and walk back, meditating on the error of your ways. The clamp is freed within one hour, and you feel curiously relieved to have been given such a gently effective lesson about unsociable street behaviour.

Would this flair for creative compromise be visible out on the polders? I had heard that the birds were spectacular, but driving across the arable prairies inland I found myself wondering whether a project that had absorbed most of Holland's natural estuaries could possibly be less damaging than coastal development back home. More than thirty British estuaries are currently endangered by nuclear power stations, tidal barrages, marinas, bunded reservoirs and the like. The fear is that, with the meeting between land and water made into something much more abrupt, the teeming natural life of the mudflats would vanish.

The Dutch response to this conundrum is simple: if the original mudflats have to go, make new ones. Flevoland, some ten miles east of Amsterdam, is the most recent area to have been materialised out of the Ijsselmeer. Of its 100,000 hectares, half is farmland and a quarter residential. The remainder is given over to nature reserves, wild areas and deciduous woodland.

Out on Flevoland's polders we were able to hold on to our scepticism – just – at the hordes of black-tailed godwits, greylag geese and roe deer grazing on the fully drained land; but not when we came to the edge of the salt-water lakes that are next in line for drainage. The wind made it difficult to venture outside the car, but it had also blown in great numbers of sea duck seeking shelter. Rafts of smew, goldeneye, scaup and merganser bobbed on the lee of the breakwater. Little gulls wafted over male goosanders – a striking contrast of fugitive dark underwing and swaggering peach bulk when a shaft of sunlight caught the two species together.

On the landward side of Flevoland's coast there is an extensive tract of reed-marsh and brackish lagoons. Marsh harriers were hunting over the willow scrub and reeds, and flocks of avocets and godwits scurried about the mud. The variety of habitats is partly due to the way the Dutch drain these areas. They are first banked, pumped partially dry, then sown (from a plane!) with reed seeds to dry them out further, and finally dyked and drained. But in the areas scheduled to be nature reserves, much of the land is left in the reed-marsh stage, though there are large stretches of mud which look as if they are managed for a slightly tidal regime, and which that day were dotted with dunlin and knot.

None of this, of course, is an exact replacement for natural estuaries. There isn't yet the intricate tracery of creeks, or the magic of a landscape made anew twice daily. Yet in one way, that is precisely the point. Estuaries aren't fixed, irreplaceable habitats like ancient woods. They are intrinsically unstable and mobile, and always have the potential of recreating themselves on the seaward side of any development – if they are given the room.

The whole of the north Norfolk marshlands, fed by just four small rivers and yet of international importance, were under the sea 500 years ago, and have emerged entirely naturally. Every year they change a little as creeks silt up or a sea wall breaches. The flats survive not by the rivers sullenly insisting on one fixed route to the sea, but by nimbly winding their way past obstacles. It's a lesson in natural flexibility that has not been lost on the Dutch, either ecologically or politically. The last time their engineers came to Britain they began the process which was to destroy most of our wetlands. I hope we may ask them back soon to help find ways of extending what remains.

There is no more agreeably green city than Oxford, especially in the spring. Where else can you wander, free of charge, among forty mazy and entirely individual parks and gardens in less than a square mile, pick medlars in the street and see a herd of fallow deer and a meadow purple with snakeshead fritillaries only a couple of hundred yards from the main through-road? Oxford is so thoroughly infused with greenery that half the time it is impossible to say what is wild and what is cultivated. Relics of old monastic gardens and donnish collections spring up through any unguarded seam (Oxford ragwort went one better and escaped to become one of the nation's most successful weeds). Sparrowhawks jink along the punt routes and over the college walls, which themselves are adorned with extraordinary mixtures of escaped herbs, seedling trees and prize roses.

That all of this has survived seems more remarkable when you remember that, as well as being a university town, Oxford is the birthplace of the mass-produced motor car. At one time it looked as if the city might be suffocated by its local Frankenstein's monster, and in 1948 Thomas Sharp published his historic report *Oxford Replanned*. It was a landmark in the appreciation of 'the spirit of place' and of the contribution that nature makes to this in a city. Yet its attitude towards the car makes one wonder if we have made any progress since. Sharp, though no friend of the car, would not challenge it, and he proposed to ease the terrible traffic congestion in the High with a relief road driven smack through Merton and Christ Church meadows, the green heart of Oxford and one of the most glorious views in England. Fortunately (especially since the ancient trees that were to ennoble the edges of 'Merton Mall' all died of Dutch elm disease twenty years later) the scheme was rejected. Instead Oxford decided simply to make things difficult for motor vehicles, with a battery of pedestrian precincts, parking restrictions, bypasses and a superlative public transport system. There is still heavy traffic at rush-hours, but it never threatens to asphyxiate the city as it did a decade or two ago.

Alas the Department of Transport shows no sign of moving in Oxford's direction. Official policy is to take the car as a fixed, sacrosanct entity, and design the rest of the environment around it. Just a few days after the approval of the new Winchester bypass, which will cut a 400-foot-wide gash through the ancient turf of Twyford Down, the Prime Minister made her notorious attack on 'airy-fairy' environmentalists in which she defined modern Britain as 'the great car economy'. What vision! Britain as a nation of garage-keepers, the Venice of the trunk roads.

I enjoy the freedom a car gives as much as anybody, but the conventional assumption that most car-owners would be horrified by any legal restriction on the size, design and use of vehicles is preposterous. We might make a start by redesigning the image of the car and making it less brutally individualistic and inimical to other life forms. I once read a learned paper which discussed the mosses which lived on half-timbered Morrises; and one field ecologist of my acquaintance has a semi-natural grassland under his accelerator pedal that is close to SSSI status. The fully developed organic car-about-town could be wonderfully chic: small, slow, adorned with hanging plant-baskets, bird-tables, and a parasol instead of a sun-roof. Traffic jams would become a real pleasure, like gently moving outdoor cafés.

Britain's trees, the press has been trumpeting, are in a state of terminal crisis. Racked by hurricanes and drought, poisoned by acid rain, millions are shedding their leaves months before time and giving up the ghost. A United Nations report has just rated our tree population the sixth worst afflicted in Europe. It is like the spectre of Dutch elm disease writ large, an ominous and premature new Fall . . .

Readers may remember an outbreak of similarly bleak prophecies during the drought summer of 1976 (when many defoliated beech and birch trees were felled in the mistaken belief that they were dead), and again during 1989. I wondered then if the state of a tree's foliage was really a reliable guide to its health. The shedding of leaves (or the development of unusually small ones) is a perfectly natural response by shallow-rooting species to drought conditions, a way of reducing water loss by transpiration. It is equally normal to find tree foliage in a state of disarray by mid-summer because of weather damage and predation. Indeed it would be a sign of sinister ecological goings-on if this were *not* so, as it would mean some catastrophe had befallen the leaf-feeding insects, with consequences that would reverberate right up the food-chain.

No one would dispute that the last few seasons have been very stressful for many tree species. An unprecedented orgy of bark-stripping by grey squirrels this spring has been the last straw for young beech trees already weakened by three years of drought, and has pointed up the folly of imposing such huge monocultures of this tree across southern England. London's planes (another virtual monoculture) are widely stricken by a fungus disorder, though this may not be terminal. And along the edges of motorways and trunk roads all kinds of species are showing the cumulative results of root damage, over-use of salt last winter and exhaust pollution.

But to lump all these incidents together as some kind of generalised 'tree crisis' is to run the risk of obscuring the complicated factors at work in each case. In a big city such as London, for instance, trees are at risk from a whole range of barely connected factors, not least of which is – still – the hostility of some ratepayers. The reasons given to council tree officers by householders wishing to cut trees down paint a depressing, tragi-comic picture of our supposed new mood of green enlightenment: 'Trees cause rats.' 'I hear the roots under the property.' 'Pine cones and branches may fall on my chihuahua.' 'Trees produce carbon dioxide and can poison you when you are asleep.'

No sooner have we begun to grasp that trees are the air-conditioners of the planet, that in cities they filter out soot, dampen noise and calm the natives, than the old miserly superstitions return: trees are too dangerous, too dirty, too long-lived to be allowed free rein in a civilised metropolis. Or, you may hear, just too fragile. A whole mythology about their imagined frailty has meant that the trees which are officially encouraged in London are a dour and monotonous bunch. The plane janes especially have become as ubiquitous and predictable as sugar beet in East Anglia.

Plane trees look absolutely right amongst the white buildings and fierce light of southern Europe. But in London, with uncertain skies and looming grey backcloths, their dense leafage can be almost funereal. Yet they continue to be planted in the belief that their tolerance of pollution (thanks to leathery, drip-dry leaves) makes them uniquely suitable as city trees. No one seems to have reckoned on the impact of root-borne salt, or the boon which street after street of a single species provides for the spread of disease.

There are plenty of better models for city trees – the locust tree, *Robinia pseudoacacia*, whose airy, acacia-like leaves give a real touch of the Mediterranean to certain streets in the Greek quarter of Bloomsbury. Or the floppy, lime-green leaves of the big catalpa by St James's Church, Piccadilly, which really shows up the moroseness of plane shade. This is arguably the best tree in London, especially when its flowers are out and smelling of sweet-peas. It is neither a victim nor a producer of 'poison', and to my knowledge has never dropped so much as a twig on a passing chihuahua.

There are trees, native and exotic, sprouting of their own accord in every waste patch, too: birch and willow in pavement cracks and National Car Park borders, figs and fruit trees on old walls. And during the last prolonged dustmen's strike a seedling tree of heaven was seen rising defiantly out of a lidless bin. Sadly, we rarely permit these embryo, wild trees to survive, and maybe one link between the various threats to trees in London and the country as a whole is the assumption that trees are a kind of pet or domestic retainer, to be chivvied, fussed over, disciplined, and given almost anything but freedom and respect.

Constable's paintings give glimpses of what our treescape was like last century. His pictures are full of recognisable trees – native black poplars, alders, ashes and the East Anglian suckering elm (currently surviving rather better than the rest of the family). The most fascinating feature of a recent exhibition [1991] is the inclusion of many of the painter's oil sketches alongside the 'finished' works. Constable began doing full-size sketches in oils, in the field, around 1812. It was a deliberate decision that had spectacular results. The sketches catch the furious energy of shifting banks of foliage and cloud, and the mercurial play of sunlight on moving water. Of course, there are exquisitely observed details in the final works – the pale flash of a house martin's rump over a dark mill-pond; the grip of a rider's heels against a horse – but it is the raw sketches that contain the essence of his innovative genius and his commitment to 'nature . . . the fountainhead, the source from which all originality must spring'. The countryside of Constable's oil sketches is light-years from the serene, sentimental 'landskip' to which his work has been reduced in countless pieces of bric-a-brac (and, it has to be said, in some of his finished pictures too). It is living, dynamic, constantly changing. And so are its trees. Constable's ashes, oaks, elms and willows might well be looked on askance by UN bureaucrats. They flay in the wind, shed leaves, lose branches and whole tops, go stag-headed, fall over, sprout horizontally. His robust defence of his open-air style could just as well be a paean for the unpampered tree: 'My art flatters nobody by imitation . . . it courts nobody by *smoothness*, it tickles nobody by *petiteness*, it is without either *fal de dal*, or *fiddle de dee*, how then can I hope to be popular?'

Hedges, too, are suffering from a surfeit of tidiness. The widespread assumption amongst land managers is that a hedge is a hedge is a hedge, and that, virtually by definition, there is just one way of maintaining them: the combination of coppicing and large-scale basket-weaving known as hedge-laying. We pay little attention to the origins and local character of hedges, or to their hugely varied interior landscapes of creepers, pollards, blossom, nut hoards and old nests.

I wonder how much we are prisoners of our own language here? The word 'hedge' is a basic unit of description, a natural metaphor for all kinds of other barriers. It first appeared as 'hegge' – a row of bushes or trees, plain and simple – in Old English texts in the eighth century. By the fourteenth century it was beginning to signify other sorts of defence, evasion and hiding. Five hundred years of being hedged in, hedged about and hedging our bets may have inclined us to take too basic and undifferentiated a view of those lines drawn across the fields.

So I have come to the Chess valley in Buckinghamshire, resolved to look into the heart of some ancient hedges, to feel their pulse. There is a string of one-time water meadows here that slope down to the river, divided up by straggling hedges that probably date from the time the meadows were still deliberately flooded to promote spring grass growth. Now the meadows are used as paddocks and marsh marigolds fill the old irrigation channels.

The hedges are about ten metres across and as many tall. They are mainly hazel but all kinds of other species are crowding in at the edges and advancing out into the meadow. I can't remember them ever being cut, and they seem to have none of the horizontal branching that would signify they had once been laid. They are more like thin copses, linear thickets, than conventional hedges.

Yet this, I realise, is also a generalised, hedges-as-scenery view. I wriggle in through the thorn skirts to see how they work at close quarters. They are almost triple hedges – two broken lines of entirely self-sown blackthorn, rose and bramble forming just clear of the shade of the central row of hazels. The hazel stools themselves are massive, and, because of browsing and the reciprocal competition from the thorn belts, are sending up new poles at their *sides*. The gaps between the hazels seem to be slowly closing, and the hedge seems to be effectively managing itself.

The first hedge I explore is by no means pure hazel. There is spindle, guelder rose, bullace and woodland hawthorn between the main bushes, and clumps of bluebell and wood anemone in the shady corridors on either side. The next has even more woody species – alder, hornbeam and holly. I imagine they may have begun as strips of natural riverine woodland left when the meadows were first cleared, coppiced occasionally, and are now returning to their origins. No doubt they will have to be restrained eventually, otherwise they will take over the meadows entirely. But to restrain them by a technique as drastic and regimenting as laying would destroy all their texture. They already have a wonderfully rich and seemingly self-regulating structure, with animal communities to match. Badgers have setts between the rows, lesser whitethroats nest in the blackthorn tangles, and I have seen hawfinches feeding in the hornbeams.

The following week I am driving back from Shropshire and finding it hard to keep my eyes on the road. Pairs of buzzards are wheeling and diving in courtship rituals along the Welsh borders. The first film of green is showing on every kind of hedge: tall lime avenues, self-sown wisps along park palings, untrimmed farm hedges snowflaked with early blackthorn blossom. I think of the multitude of ways that hedges were formed in the past, spontaneously colonising the edges of wattle 'dead hedges', for instance, or set by burying bundles of straw filled with nuts and fruits. Almost nothing was frowned on. In an eighteenth-century farming book I have read precise instructions for creating a hedge of elder, economically valuable then for its crops of flowers, berries and carvable rootstock.

I pass into the duller realm of well-laid Midland quicksets, and wonder if there are hedge-nesting buzzards anywhere in the kingdom. Perhaps clinging on in the big beech windbreaks round

Exmoor, where the indiscriminate march of hedge-laying is already turning some of those great hedges into suburban topiary . . . ?

It appeared in April, tiptoeing between the rose bushes – a youngish muntjac deer, with a splendid white scut. Muntjacs escaped from Woburn Park in the 1880s and since then have become thoroughly naturalised in the Chilterns. You can often glimpse them in ones or twos, diminutive creatures about the size of an alsatian, strolling through the bigger gardens and allotments. But I have never seen one behave so openly and confidingly in such a comparatively small garden – and in broad daylight, too.

It chewed its way meditatively along the borders, coming so close to the house that I was able to do an intimate survey of muntjac food preferences. It relished plantain, ivy, hazel leaves, bramble, and some rather unusual geranium species. It rejected daphnes, foxgloves and all kinds of bulbous shoots – though not before it had passed its lips over the leaves, the ungulate equivalent, no doubt, of keying a species out. But above all it adored the young foliage of old-fashioned roses, and we are not going to see much blossom below the browse line this summer. I consoled myself by thinking that it had really just eaten the excess I had failed to prune in the winter, and admired its good taste in spending so long nibbling my name rose, *Rosa richardii*.

Then the cats discovered it. Our one-year-old, Pip (so called because he began life looking more like a small pipistrelle bat than a kitten), was first on the scene. Pip is, thankfully, too much of a clown and exhibitionist acrobat to be any good as a hunter, but he is resolutely curious and trusting. He slithered up to the muntjac on his stomach, and they rubbed noses briefly before springing back in mutual surprise at what they had done. Then the entire neighbourhood cat gang arrived, and took it in turns to gaze in astonishment, stalk, sniff and shake a paw. The muntjac seemed quite unperturbed by this, and went on chewing roses between the odd nod and sniff in return. Only when the cats' attention became too intense did it occasionally shape up for a mock butt, or leap *backwards*, which paradoxically seemed to have a much more chastening effect.

It stayed for two days and rested up in a kind of form under the yew tree. And while it ruminated on exotic rose cud, up to half a dozen cats would be perched at various distances round it, becoming just as relaxed themselves. The scene reminded me of one of those Renaissance paintings of Eden before the Fall, and was wonderful to contemplate after months of witnessing humans being decidedly red in tooth and claw. On the third day it was gone, and the cat troupe went back to their current craze of leaping balletically after gnats.

During a spell of fine weather in early summer, when the winds were blowing in continuously from the continent, Britain was invaded by waves of exotic migrants. Bee-eaters flickered about the south coast, and carillons of golden orioles sang on the Isle of Wight. The West Country, on Birdline's recorded daily bulletins, sounded increasingly like the Camargue, with black-winged stilts, woodchat shrikes and purple herons loafing in the Cornish marshes. Red-footed falcons patrolled the skies above eastern England. At Stodmarsh in Kent, there were four at once, hunting with hobbies in a display of aerial power that must have made the local swallows wish they had never left Africa.

I heard too late about the flock of eight cattle egrets that had arrived improbably on a Hertfordshire gravel pit, just fifteen minutes' drive from my home. They wafted in from their breeding grounds in north Africa, and a few days later wafted away again. I appeased myself by saying that I wasn't really a twitcher anyway – a blatant piece of self-deception. When I heard that some of the flock had turned up at the Ouse Washes, only a short detour from a trip I was making anyway, I was there with my telescope like the rest.

It was worth it. There were five birds in the flock, feeding and striking poses in a rough pasture by the side of the A1101, and they proved to be the most handsome and obliging of creatures, spending much of the time within forty or fifty yards of the road. Every so often one would fly a short distance to a new feeding or idling spot, with that deliciously nonchalant flight style that egrets have – so much billowy white wing that they seem to be being blown along like scraps of stray sheeting. Three of them had the distinctive buff plumes on crown and breast that is part of the species' breeding plumage.

They shared the field with a herd of Friesians and looked thoroughly at home, poking around for food close to the feet of the meandering cattle exactly as they do by the Mediterranean. The cows were less familiar with this symbiotic arrangement though, and every so often would make half-hearted charges. One even tried to butt an egret into a dyke. The birds were unperturbed and continued to give their practical lessons in coexistence.

Despite their promising plumage (and, apparently, a perceptible northerly expansion of the species' breeding range) they didn't stay and try to nest. But for a few warm and congenial days they provided a startling tableau of the surprise and vitality of nature. I do hope they got home safely.

One of the ironies of natural catastrophes is that the more spectacular they are the less likely you are to witness them at close quarters. I am relieved that self-preservation has so far got the better of my perverse yearning to glimpse a group of big trees going over in a gale. But personal comfort is an altogether feebler excuse, and next time there is a deluge anything like the monsoon rains which hit the home counties again this summer [1992] I think I will go out and brave it.

The worst of the storms in mid-June caused extraordinary mayhem in the Chilterns. Even the most gently sloping roads ended in a tide-wrack of gravel and unsavoury detritus forced up through the drain covers. Drifts of flints and stones sluiced out of the fields were deep enough to block off some of the hollow lanes. On one particularly steep and twisting lane, the torrents had burrowed underneath the road, wrenched out chunks of tarmac and tossed them down the hill.

We tend to think of floods chiefly in terms of the damage they do to homes and farmland, and it hadn't occurred to me that similarly awesome events might have been taking place in my wood. Hardings Wood is full of eccentric slopes and zig-zag paths and is, I can see now, a kind of adventure playground for free-range water. But I hadn't anticipated the liberties the flood would take, and certainly not the discovery, fifty yards down the entrance track, of banks of woodland flotsam – beech mast, dock stems, last year's leaves – looking like the remains of a serious East Coast flood-tide. The water had rasped through the wood, cutting miniature channels along the main tracks, down to the bare flint in places. Everywhere it had taken short cuts. It had burst through a hedge from the adjacent field, got stuck in a dam of its own making, detoured down a few badger paths, abandoned the winding track and taken off straight down the hill.

In the dry valley that runs through the heart of the wood, there looked as if there had been something resembling a tidal wave. Water running into this gully from three different directions had built up into a torrent that had torn huge clumps of fern out by the roots and shrivelled nettle leaves up to a height of eighteen inches. It had also broken off a six-inch-thick branch from a fallen tree and driven it forward like a snow-plough, wiping a swath of ground forty feet long and six feet wide quite clear of vegetation.

I'd often felt that there should be a stream in this valley. No doubt there was once, and what I missed on the night of the June storm was the sight of water flowing along the same ancestral pathways it had cut 15,000 years ago, as the glaciers melted away.

It was altogether more clement weather when I drove up to Norfolk for the Forestry Commission's (FC) census of singing nightjars in Thetford Forest. The swifts were black over Brandon; the avenue of lime-trees leading up to the FC's headquarters at Santon Downham was roaring with bees; and the Breckland flowers looked sensational.

This vast sand bowl has always been good for nightjars, but since the FC began clear-felling its pine plantations (mostly dating from just after the First World War) Breckland has become the British stronghold of this species. They prefer the felled and recently replanted areas to even prime heathland sites, and are so dense in some compartments that it would be hard not to hear some.

But I was still glad to have as my guide Ron Hoblyn, who has been the FC's conservation officer for the Forest for twenty years. As we had a few hours of daylight before the birds would start churring, he took me on an unexpected treat – to see two occupied nightjar nests. We drove through miles of sculpted pine clumps and flowery plains which looked – and smelt – more like Provence than the stereotype of an FC conifer estate. Nearly half the entire Forest is now more or less open, and twenty per cent is going to remain permanently unplanted. The rides and clearings were filled with spectacular ribbons of blue viper's bugloss and yellow weld. Families of young woodlarks rose up from dust-bathing on the tracks, and roe-deer leaped across them.

The first nest was on a bare patch of ground at the foot of a ten-year-old pine. There had been two eggs, but there was only one chick, a beautiful candy-striped thing, which sat tucked up and perfectly still. The mother was circling and calling anxiously round our heads, so we didn't stay long. At the second, set in a vestigial clearing in the bracken, the hen bird was sitting tight. We kept our distance, and Ron had to point the bird out to me, so perfectly did its patchwork plumage blend in with the background of dry bracken and old leaves.

Ron told me that as numbers (and presumably family lineages) build up in the Forest, so the birds become less fussy about their nest sites. He has found nests among grass tussocks, on top of pine stumps and even in a clump of heath bedstraw. All the birds seem to require is a little bare earth, a dead branch or two, and a few trees for perching and singing.

There were more than a hundred people from bird-watching groups and local villages in the Forest that night, and they logged more than 300 churring males. Ron and I heard five on our beat, including one tireless but hiccupy bird which, performing from high in a pine, treated us to a wonderful display of insect-catching aerobatics round the very top of the tree.

I was there just five hours, but it was an intoxicating evening: the great sweeps of the reopened landscape, the smells of hot gorse and pine sap, the hypnotic reeling of the jars, Ron Hoblyn's remarkable insights into this mysterious East Anglian desert.

The return of the nightjars to Thetford Forest is, by itself, one of the great bird success stories. But the FC, first by accident and now by design, seems to be returning much of the landscape to the wild, sporadically cultivated, open steppe-land it was in Neolithic times. I shall be back.

It proved to be a magnificent summer in southern France, too, especially for butterflies. Down in the limestone hills west of the Cevennes, a sharp-eyed acquaintance logged more than seventy species in a fortnight. I was camping there in August with some old friends and their children – Francesca Greenoak and John Kilpatrick, and Robin and Rachel Hamilton. They are devoted naturalists all, but not in the least bit solemn, and as the array of butterfly species – Cleopatra, Satyr, Dryad – began to resemble the cast of a Greek drama, so, doped silly by the afternoon heat, we fantasised our own lists of theatrical sun-flies: the True Blue, the Bent Copper, the Grey-rinsed Skipper (or Old Heath) and the Large White Supremacist (*Eugenia terreblanchea*).

This was alternative humour showing its middle age, but it did underline for me what a great source of shared metaphors and memories the natural world is. My friends earn part of their keep by running guided walks for other campers. But these familiar rambles are important rituals for us too, a way of beating our tribal bounds and saluting old friends: the dippers, lizards and lilies along the wooded river walk to Nant (and *citron pressé* under the village arches); the feathery limestone grass, *Stipa pennata*, like the trail left by a sparkler at night, up on top of the radio-mast cliff. One evening we always go to hear nightjars on a high *causse* to the west. This year we were almost past their breeding season, but in one magical moment a pair skimmed down – silent, weightless spectres in the half-light – to hover and drink in a dew pond.

There were new experiences, too. The heat, for one, which in early August is stunning. Feeling more at ease than I have for years, I sleep outside, gazing at the shooting stars and listening to the poignant creaks of the children swinging in their hammocks. (They have been making an *un*-nature trail, hanging strings of garlic in trees, and moulding bird-of-paradise droppings out of striped toothpaste.) One afternoon we go swimming in the Dourbie, my first river-dip for decades. Moving slowly and half-covered by water we seem to be accepted by other creatures. Silver-wash fritillary and banded grayling butterflies as big as warblers fly in procession above us. Crag martins swoop lazily for water a few feet from our heads. Young viperine snakes wriggle past and, to a great cheer, one catches a striped horsefly known to us only as the Thing That Bites John.

But it is the ordinary, daily rituals that touch me most: the camp serin that at eight-thirty each morning begins the extraordinary sub-song Rachel christens its *chanson de toilette*; picking wild thyme outside the tent for the evening meal; and in the afternoons lolling in the shade of a tree with our field guides and trying to work out the plants found that day. It can be a fruitless task, wallowing amongst the beautiful profusion of the French flora. But no matter, for this ritual is also a kind of conversation, an exchange of personal whims and ways of thinking as much as an identification parade.

We all sometimes use nature like a language. Making private jokes and symbols out of it is partly a way of saying we all understand it, of cementing our bonds as a group. And maybe being, so to speak, so *familiar* with it is a way of expressing an affinity with other living things that, for all our word games, is deeper than words.

I imagine everyone has their own vivid recollections of Britain's August heat-wave: hose-pipe bans and wasp plagues; a giant Caribbean turtle gulping jellyfish in the English Channel; beech-mast so heavy that it made the leaves look as if they were brown in July; and that rare experience in Britain of heat intense enough to come close to the pain threshold.

But how long will these recollections last? Our climatic folk memory is notoriously short and erratic, and full of a gloomy mythology whose only silver lining is a vague belief in ancient Golden Summers. It is as if, living in a part of the world where the weather will always be capricious, we daren't allow ourselves the luxury of remembering *specific* weather instances for fear of developing foolhardy expectations. Who recalls the summer of 1983, which had the hottest July for 300 years? Or of 1975, which started on 6 June after snowfalls on the 2nd and stretched to the end of August? (And hands up all those who are thinking 'Surely he means 1976?' – a heat-wave universally remembered, with typical British masochism, because it led to a drought.)

I hope I'm not being smug. I doubt if I would remember them myself if I hadn't kept a weather diary for twenty years. I certainly can't imagine what my abiding image of this year's heat-wave would turn into if I hadn't written it down.

It was a Sunday night at the beginning of August, and too

hot for sleep. I was lying on the bed gazing idly out of the window, when the sky suddenly became full of careering balls of light. They were round and hazy and darting about in a way that made them look indisputably alive. I was mesmerised at first, then alarmed, but by the time I had summoned another member of the household as a witness they had vanished. For the next few days what I thought was a firmly rooted natural scepticism had a very rough ride indeed. I thought up every possible rationalisation. I wondered if I had witnessed a bizarre electric storm or a giant corn circle being formed, or in fact was suffering from heat-stroke and had witnessed nothing at all. But it was the way the lights moved – purposefully and randomly all at once – that dogged me. I could not get out of my mind that this kind of patterning could only be associated with living things. I toyed desperately with the possibility that they might have been bats which had picked up phosphorescence in their roosts, as barn owls sometimes do.

Four days later the local paper saved me from panic, if not embarrassment. The lights had been seen all over the area, and had come not from UFOs or luminous bats but from a laser show at a Tina Turner rock concert at Woburn Park, more than fifteen miles away.

All summer the tousled sweeps of Tring Park had seemed to be thickening, like a cat's new coat. I'd catch glimpses of it from the bypass, and even from a distance could see the tide of young ash rising in the storm-blasted beech hangers and new shoots seeping up through the tawny stems of last year's ungrazed grasses. The whole prospect stirred perceptibly in the breeze. Something was going on in there.

It is a spectacular place, but I had stayed clear recently while it weathered one of its periodic crises. Back in the seventeenth century it was the north-west tip of Tring common, a tract of woodland, grass and heath that stretched over more than 3,000 acres. But gradually it was eaten away, one slice appropriated for a private park in the mid-eighteenth century, more for plantation woods, the last 300 acres filched and enclosed by Parliamentary enactment in 1853. The parkland area became grazing land and an unofficial public open space after the war, but a few years ago it was bought by Whitbread, who had ambitions to turn it into a golf course and country club. Fortunately it lies in the Chilterns' Area of Outstanding Natural Beauty, and the brewery's original schemes were summarily turned down by the planning authorities. So for the last eighteen months it has been a brooding and deliciously unkempt waste, getting its breath back.

I gave in to its new charms in June. I had just been to visit the Chilterns' soldier orchid site, and had been delighted by the spreading colonies which are no longer barricaded off, as they were in the 1970s. I remembered that Tring Park was probably one of the orchid's last Hertfordshire sites in the nineteenth century, when it grew 'abundantly' in sunny places by the edges of chalky woods, and I had a wild fancy that it might just have reappeared in the tangled west-facing slopes. Needless to say, I didn't find any, but the whole place had an invigorating sense of profusion. There were drifts of cowslips in seed, enough salad burnet to stain the steeper slopes claret and, in the half-shade along the wood-edge, a glimmering brocade of bugle and jasmine-scented valerian.

Then I began to hear the stories of the barn owls, which have not bred in this corner of the country for maybe twenty years. There were sightings by the village allotments, and one spotted on a path, munching a vole. They were all centred around Tring Park.

I took to going for dusktime walks amongst the overgrown paddocks and ragged hedges that lie between my wood and the Park. I didn't see the barn owls, but the smell of hay, the feel of rough grass on bare legs, and the low sun striping the beechwoods with shadows, conjured up the most powerful memories of enchanted evening walks as a teenager and of school holidays running wild as a boy. Our playground then was also an abandoned park, part of a long-demolished mansion. There were barn owls nesting in the old stables and they patrolled the lines of poplars and crumbling walls that marked our common boundaries.

Then, one evening in July, feeling lucky after watching two of the Chilterns' red kites circling a village further south, I stopped off for a quick look at the Park. It was about eight-fifteen, and I saw the owls immediately, quartering the bleached, thigh-high grass that was now dotted with orchids and scabious, and the moon-discs of hogweed flowers. They were diving for prey roughly every thirty seconds, and catching something on about one strike in ten. I kept low and edged in the direction they were ferrying the food. They seemed quite unperturbed by my presence, so much so that I began to wonder if barn owls had slight tunnel vision. So when one flew straight towards me, I stood my ground. It sheared off with a screech when it was about twenty metres away, and went and hid in a tree. I hid too, in a hedge, and then followed them more discreetly to the nest tree, which proved to be an ancient beech with half its top blown out. Burying myself in a drift of hogweed nearby, I had the magical experience of the owls wafting past me just feet away, as silent as a breath.

I went back to the Park often over the summer, and each time the owls came out to hunt a little later. And each time I glimpsed, for just a few maddening seconds, the silhouette of a third owl. I thought at first that it was an unusually plumaged barn owl, but am now convinced that it was a short- or long-eared owl, which would be a testament indeed to the teeming mammal life in this Chiltern pampas. My last visit was on a moonless night before the rains began. It was almost too dark to see, but I could just make out the adult owls dancing around amongst the branches, and I guess the young were on the point of leaving the nest.

One day, I suppose, the Park will have to be managed, other-wise it will all turn into woodland within a couple of decades (though all it really needs is a hurricane once a century and an occasional passing herd of bison). But I hope whoever has charge of it will have seen it this summer in its prime, with the wild woods tumbling into the valley, and the owls beating over a mile of waving grass that looked less like tame old England than the Elysian plains of John Muir's California, before the ranchers came.

What forager could resist the lure of a four-day *Festa de fungho* in Tuscany, one of Europe's richest mushroom-hunting grounds? The banners hung enticingly all round the villages east of Arezzo, and I could imagine the scene: the trestle tables piled with ceps (the Italians call them *porcini*, 'little pigs'); the tasting and identification sessions, the chance maybe to swap schoolboy Latin with fellow enthusiasts and find out where on earth the things were lurking. There seemed to be plenty in the markets, and in the hill town of Lucignano we had been tantalised by an extraordinary, almost primitive, thirteenth-century fresco in which St Francis was receiving the stigmata (from what looked like laser beams) on a hillside covered with plump *porcini*. But wherever we searched this early September the ground looked too parched to support a blade of grass let alone a fungus. When we arrived on the opening day the *festa* proved to have as much to do with fungi as our latter-day harvest festivals have to do with wheat. It was just an autumn fair with a symbolic seasonal tag, and amidst the bars and disco tents there was not a mushroom, edible or otherwise, to be seen.

There is something of the same sense of illusion about the Tuscan countryside as a whole. It must be one of the best known prospects in the world, and that skyline of warm brown hills, terraced with olives and vines and studded with ragged lines of cypress trees, has been celebrated in paintings as a kind of idealised pastoral landscape, a model of harmony between man and nature, for the past 800 years.

It looks just as spectacular in the flesh – at least from a distance. What surprised me was just how uncompromisingly intensive the local agriculture is when seen close-to. The terracotta hills, which I had always assumed to be covered by sun-bleached grass, are blanket-ploughed – up impossible slopes, over sharp ridges and tumps, and often right up to the edges of the road. Even the vineyards are often ploughed between the vines. There is little grazing land, and arable crops dominate the scene: tobacco, maize and especially sunflowers. Waste corners are about as common as they are in East Anglia, and, with farmsteads every few hundred yards, there isn't much sense of wildness in the landscape.

Of course there are exceptions. There are oakwoods higher up the hills (though few old trees) and plenty of enterprising smallholdings. And everywhere there are echoes of the inventive and frugal cultivation methods that were pioneered here 4,000 years ago. We saw vines trained, permaculture-style, up other fruit trees, cherries especially, and pumpkins and melons draped down the slopes between olive terraces.

There was a profusion of insects, too, even in the most thronging tourist spots. I saw my first Camberwell Beauty in a car park and a swallowtail dithering along one of the narrow alleyways that lead up to the great central square (Il Campo) in Siena. Hummingbird hawkmoths hunted the hotel fuchsia baskets, and the crickets were cacophonous everywhere, every night.

Yet the overriding impression was of a tight, over-organised landscape, made eerie by a dearth of birds. There were no tits scrumping the ripening sunflower seeds, no lark or finch flocks on the stubbles, no woodpeckers in the oak woods, no crag martins in the hill villages and not one single bird of prey anywhere, although the hot weather was ideal for them. Most ominously there were not even any bird corpses on the roads. In seven days I saw the dismal and barely credible total of eighteen species, mostly, except for feral pigeons, sparrows and swallows (the latter were far and away the commonest and most visible species), as single birds.

I know a hot early September is not a good time for birds even in Britain. They are often moulting or migrating, and keeping a low profile. Yet I have never experienced a landscape so drained of the life and vitality that wild birds normally provide so generously, and found it hard not to think that the Italians' obsessional desire to shoot anything that flies must have something to do with it. (We were there for the beginning of the season, and heard the first shots at two minutes after midnight.) Have whole lineages of resident birds been exterminated or exiled or driven into hiding by generations of persecution – leaving the constantly replenished streams of migrants to play the hapless role of cannon-fodder?

There were more clues in the abundance of medieval artwork that adorns churches and civic buildings throughout Tuscany. We saw no fewer than three thirteenth-century paintings in one village which showed the infant Jesus firmly clasping a live swallow, suggesting that it may have been a privileged species, a bringer of grace and good fortune for centuries. And in Siena one of the first panoramic pictures of a rural scene, painted by Ambrogio Lorenzetti in 1338, shows a Tuscan landscape almost identical to the one that survives today. It is a reminder, perhaps, that a diverse, even organic, farming landscape may not automatically be accommodating to nature.

It is more than two decades since I wrote my first nature book, a guide to edible wild plants called *Food For Free*. It was a modest success in its own way, enabling me to risk becoming a full-time freelance, and I shall always be grateful for that.

But it had also the kind of oddball subject matter that gets one typecast. A few years after publication I was introduced to a well-known photographer at a party. 'Ah yes,' he mused, peering closely at me. 'You're the man that eats weeds. What an interestingly *earthy* face.' This, I felt, shrinking with embarrassment, was taking the idea that you are what you eat a little too literally, and ever since I have distanced myself slightly from that early guide to greens. I still enjoy feasts of seasonal crops: samphire from the north Norfolk marshes in summer, wild raspberries from my own wood, local hazelnuts for Christmas. But for the most part I have become a rather precious wayside nibbler, indulging in what the 1930s writer and fruit gourmet Edward Bunyard christened 'ambulant consumption' – single wild gooseberries (squeezed to test for ripeness first), sweet cicely seeds on walks before dinner as a kind of herbal aperitif, squidgy dewberries eaten on the stalk, like cocktail cherries.

This year, however, with an anniversary to celebrate and an odd pattern of weather whose effects on normal fruiting patterns I was curious to explore, I felt inclined to go for a proper, inquisitive foray, a working lunch, so to speak.

So I map out a route over familiar country near home which takes in some old hedges and one-time mushroom pastures, hoist a gathering bag over my shoulder – and then curse the fact that the mid-October day that I have carefully planned for this expedition turns out to be the most dismal of the autumn so far.

But half a mile on I find I am quite enjoying the mist and fine drizzle. The berries on the trees, dust washed off at last, have an inviting dewy sheen. On the grassland, now thoroughly mois- tened, patches and rings of darker green grass that may be signs of underground fungal growth are materialising like watermarks.

I start browsing out of a sense of duty to begin with, and drench myself with showers of settled rainwater every time I reach into a bush. Things are already remarkably ripe, even though there have been no air frosts yet. I nibble a few agreeably soft haws, whose flesh always reminds me of underripe avocado, then start on the blackberries, which are still swelling in good numbers, despite all those saws about not picking them after Michaelmas. Even berries from adjacent bushes can taste quite different, with hints of grape, cherry, plum, and subtly different textures, reminding you that there are 400 microspecies of bramble in Britain.

But I draw a blank with hazelnuts. It was not a good year for them to start with, and this year's explosion in grey squirrel numbers seems to have put paid to the few that did form. I try a few tricks, such as getting inside the bushes and looking out, hoping that any clusters will be more visible against the sky. But all I find are a few rather stale cobs already fallen to the ground. I munch some elderberries for consolation, but overdo it, and that slight cloying sensation, of having sucked fruit-flavoured frog-spawn, won't go away. There are clusters of miniature wood puffballs on the tree stumps, though, and I find that chewing some of the white flesh takes the elder aftertang away.

My route takes me up into the Chiltern foothills, and a labyrinth of green lanes. Long-tailed tits are dithering through the hedges, and the first chaffinch flocks gathering – though there is no beech mast either for them or me. I am heading for a wilding apple tree I discovered last year – sniffed out, actually, since its lemon-yellow fruits smelt deliciously of quince and scented the air for dozens of yards around. (They were too hard and acid to eat raw, but were spectacular roast with meat.) The tree has fruited quite well again, though it is too early for the fruits to have taken on their heady aroma. But there are plenty of other wilding apples about. I bite into one and it has the bitter-sweet, almost effervescent zest of sherbet. On another tree in the same hedge they are like miniature pippins. A third has long pear-shaped apples that have an extraordinary warm, smoky flavour behind the sharpness, as if they had already been baked. I ponder the huge genetic storehouse represented by these wayside wildings, all sprung from discarded cores and maybe cross-bred with true crab apples.

But I must be disappointed at how few fungi there are in the hedges and copses, as I start hallucinating them. A promising mound under an oak turns out to be a toy bubble car, and every white flash in the field is eventually an upturned flint. But as I turn for home through the valley meadows, with rooks massing above the woods on either side, I begin to strike lucky. There are freshly sprung field mushrooms, pink-gilled and unsullied by insects. There are fairy rings of eight-inch-diameter horse-mushrooms and of shaggy parasols (no good for eating raw, but I pick a bagful for later).

And in the ridgeway hedges on the last lap before home, the wild damsons are perfectly ripe and beginning to drop from the trees. The bushes line an old orchard and were, I guess, originally planted as a combination windbreak and pollinator for the cultivated plums. But they have spread some way beyond their original site, and suckers and seedlings (including a wonderful cherry-plum with round, thick, orange fruit) crop up for hundreds of yards along the hedge. There is one new taste sensation here. The hedge was cut in the summer with the fruit already formed, and the trimmings lie beneath it, covered with dry, wrinkled damsons that taste exactly like thin-fleshed prunes.

So this was my midday meal, ambulantly consumed but in strictly correct order: young field mushrooms and a few soft chestnuts, finished with wild plums and strips of lemony apple. After three hours of continuous nibbling it seemed, I will confess, rather on the acid and insubstantial side, and I began to yearn for a bowl of pasta. But never believe anyone who says there is no such thing as a free lunch.

One of the most poignant of all medieval myths about the natural world concerns 'the vegetable lamb', an extraordinary hybrid creature, half living beast, half plant, which supposedly occurred in Tartary. The lamb grew from a bush whose ripe fruit burst open to reveal a small four-legged animal. Its 'coate or rinde is woolly like unto a Lambe's skinne', wrote the botanist John Parkinson, and 'it hath the forme of an head hanging down and feeding on the grasse round about it until it hath consumed it'. Then the stem withered, the lamb died, and the cycle began again.

It is almost certain that the myth was based on the cotton plant, which was first discovered in this part of Asia. But this hardly explains its persistence well into the seventeenth century, or the power of those evocative images. All enduring myths reflect deep-seated human fears or wonderment, and the vegetable lamb echoes with our feelings about the mysteries of transubstantiation, the frugal economics of the living world, the basic unity of plants and animals.

Another early image of nature – a cluster of Chinese boxes, each opening to reveal an exquisite new variation on its predecessor – came to mind on a trip to southern Devon in late October. It was my first visit to the luxuriant country of the South Hams, and the balmy air and newness of it all made me feel quite light-headed. Twisting down through moss-lined hedgebanks on a morning scented by warm Atlantic breezes was like driving inside a seashell. There were primroses – the last of this year or the first of the next – almost open in the grass, and red admirals sun-bathing on oak trunks. In the village of East Allington there were swallows on the wires still, and we felt we had been transported clean through winter into spring.

Gilbert White had come to this village in September 1750 to stay with the rector, his old Oxford friend Nathan Wells. It was the furthest he ever journeyed from Selborne. I don't normally put much faith in retracing old footsteps, but my companion urged me on to look at the Old Rectory, and it proved to be a revelation.

A thin stream wound seductively down from the rectory to a ragged, enfolded copse, a treasure chest of natural miniatures. There was a hollow ash pollard, with a trunk etched like the face of an ancient carp; the shell of a log packed with puffballs; a honeysuckle insinuating itself round a single frond of fern. Gilbert must have walked down here, too, and been intoxicated to find his dense, muddled Selborne landscape transplanted to the Gulf Stream.

The next day *we* were in a Chinese box, looking up at the swell of Dartmoor from the maze of woods and clapper-bridged streams west of Ashburton. On the moor itself, the air was light and frisky, with barely a hint of Baskervillian gloom. The grass was springy, the hawthorns full of redwings and fieldfares. A snipe jinked up from a thin trickle of water we did not see till we were almost in it; and, from a little further away, there came, marvellously, the lilting call of a greenshank.

That afternoon we were initiated into the arcane rituals of letter-boxing, and shown some of the thousands of little boxes, with their registers and stamps, that are now hidden under stones and in crevasses across the moor. Humans have been burrowing in Dartmoor for 4,000 years for one reason or another, and the

223

letter boxes seem a fitting modern expression of the tradition, and an emblem of the partnership that has made the intimate landscapes of south Devon. 'Natural' and 'man-made' are treacherous words to apply to places (or substances). Most of the best and most generous cleavings of humans to nature have been both, or neither; they are true hybrids, as subtle, modest, full of meaning and the possibilities of new life as the vegetable lamb.

Gruesome, freezing fogs are the latest contribution to our thickening catalogue of extreme weather. I normally enjoy a mist, especially the tantalising sense it can give you of life going on just beyond sight. But these are real miasmas, as oppressive and choking (and toxic, it turns out) as the true smogs of the 1950s.

I was in Norfolk during one of the first, when the vertical visibility was down to about forty feet. Above us we could hear the pitiful contact calls of thousands of invisible pinkfeet geese trying to locate their feeding grounds, needing, it seems, a visible groundplan as well as their directional instincts to find their way about.

A few weeks later I was just as hopelessly disorientated myself. I had rashly set out at night to drive fifty miles in the densest fog of the winter in an emergency dash home. I managed to travel four miles in an hour before the visibility dropped to about three yards, and the fog started crystallising as thin spiders' webs of ice on my windscreen. I hadn't the slightest idea of my direction, developed a migraine, then a nosebleed; and not until a pub swam out of the murk was I able to compose myself.

What happened to me and to the geese? What factors maintain a creature's sense of direction? Back in the early 1980s this looked like becoming an exciting area of collaboration between natural history and human biology. Work at Manchester University had established that humans did possess an atrophied 'sixth sense' of direction, and that it operated through magnetically sensitive tissue in the sinuses. The Dragon Project was beginning to use these findings to demystify dowsing and standing stones (an early kind of environmental sculpture). Now there is silence, and I fear the mutual hostility between conventional and fringe science has claimed another casualty.

1988–93

Epilogue

SAD – A NATURAL HISTORY OF HYPOCHONDRIA

Journals are perverse things. For as long as I've kept one, my chirpy notes on spring migrants and balmy Indian summers have been periodically interrupted by whimpering outbursts on my internal weather. In 1985, for instance: *Jan.* 7 – 'Very cold. Snow persists. Panicky, flu-like symptoms. I hate this claggy, shrivelling weather, forcing you into yourself . . .' *Jan.* 8 – 'Desperately cold night. Racked with rheumatism and anxiety . . .' *Jan.* 9 – 'Slight thaw, but still feel hemmed in.' I can remember the last time I really enjoyed the winter, but not the moment I decided these spells of malaise and *memento mori* deserved a place amongst the nature notes.

The moods and symptoms often seem to follow the course of external weather, with headaches tracking storm fronts, and low spirits in lows. But I don't think they are just forms of what is now known as SAD (seasonal affective disorder) or winter depression. Little runs of hypochondriacal fronts crop up in other seasons, and sometimes even on the same days each year, like those annually recurrent spells of weather known as Buchan's Periods. I have never had anything as spectacularly temporal as the stigmata and 'palmar migraines' that some Catholics experience every Easter; but when, for example, the spring fails to behave as it should I can become quite irrationally discomfited. If the weather hasn't turned by the beginning of May, I begin to fret. If the swifts and house martins are late, I'm nagged by fears that this may be the year they fail to make it back home. Worry can turn insidiously into anxiety, so that if the weather does improve dramatically I dash about trying to cram all the postponed spring pleasures into half a day, and end up ragged and let down. Sometimes I wonder if I ought to become a seasonal migrant myself.

I fear I am plugging into some bad old habits when this happens. I learned the power of symptoms at an unhealthily early age, especially to protest against thwarted expectations. They could grab attention, rebuke loved ones, get you out of unpleasant situations. Childhood psychosomatic complaints were, at one level, just a manifestation of sulking, radiating pitiableness and pique at the same time. But they were also attributed at that time to one's being 'highly strung', like some corporeal wind harp. I was prone to 'bad nerves' (and believing my heart had stopped in the night), to 'bilious attacks', and to what my parents called 'acidosis' (simple indigestion), which occasionally made me feel I had inflated to the size of a barrage balloon. I had lumps in the throat (Globus hystericus) and tingles in the scalp.

In my teens, these childish symptoms were replaced by more adult ones – if hypochondria can ever be described as adult. I acquired hay fever, an over-sensitive gut, and occasional mild agoraphobia. My body seemed bent on sabotaging my adolescent ambition, which was to be an outdoor adventurer, a kind of scholar gypsy. I wasn't sophisticated enough to construe the body as some sort of interface between nature and the self, but I could see that I was watching its reactions in much the same way as I did birds and insects, straining to recognise stirrings in the undergrowth and unfamiliar noises. I was also aware that most symptoms occurred when I was in unfamiliar surroundings, what John Clare called 'being out of my knowledge', and were designed to get me home, or at least to somewhere secure.

Homesickness was, intriguingly, the first meaning of nostalgia (another psychological state linked with the outdoors) and was once viewed as a serious organic complaint. It was medically diagnosed and named (from the Greek *nosos*, return to native land, and *algos*, grief) by Johannes Hofer in 1688. Hofer described the illness as 'a continuous vibration of animal spirits through those fibres of the middle brain in which the impressed traces of the idea of the Fatherland still cling'. Swiss mercenaries were apparently amongst the early victims. They would sink rapidly into depression and emaciation on hearing distant cattle bells or alpine songs that reminded them of their home pastures. As late as the Second World War, homesickness/nostalgia was on the US Surgeon General's list as a 'contagious disorder', which could spread like an epidemic through induction centres and barracks.

Psychosomatic disorder almost always has a *purpose* (in the above case to get you home) inside its extravagances. The psychologist George Groddeck thought it was less a disease than a hapless form of self-expression: 'Whoever sees in illness a vital expression of the organism will no longer see it as an enemy . . . [It] is a creation of the patient . . . the same sort of thing as his manner of walking, his facial expression.' But acceptance is more easily recommended than achieved, especially when this unconscious customising becomes wildly inventive. One modern American hypochondriac (described by Edward Shorter in *From Paralysis to Fatigue*) conjured an extraordinarily florid parade of complaints – or at least perceptions of complaints – out of the human symptom pool: 'Muscle spasms in her right leg, armpit and ribcage which increase when she walks . . . Shaking inside her spinal column and in the eye sockets . . . Skin on fire . . . The experience of her intestines rising up in her abdomen and feeling like a "banana" . . . Abnormal sensory experiences such as colours jumping out of paintings at her and brown rice vibrating on a plate . . .'

The greatest scope for improvisation is in the seething stockpot known as irritable bowel syndrome (IBS). Every kind of irregularity and embarrassing turbulence gets filed (in common understanding anyway) under this portmanteau term. It is also the base for a kind of freemasonry. When I first explained my own trivial version to a doctor, he replied with what sounded like a password.

'And how do you cope with the early-morning no-corridor train?' There is no answer to that; but IBS can bring out some canny backwoodsmanship in one's search for discreet retreats in public places. In London's Bond Street, where anything as communal as a convenience is anathema, I once begged information about the nearest gents from a newspaper seller. Without a word he marched me down the road, briefed me about an exclusive upstairs loo, and then diverted the doorkeeper of Sotheby's while I nipped up the stairs.

Even oddities that aren't 'creations of the patient' can have a distinctly personal stamp. Some time ago, at a routine check-up, I was told that I had a slight heartbeat irregularity known as the Wolff-Parkinson-White syndrome. The consultant gave me an enthralling lecture, illustrated with pencil sketches of the heart (*my* heart, that is). WPW involves an electrical leak, a short-circuit through the heart by part of the current that coordinates the pumping of the ventricles. It is normally harmless, though sometimes sets up a kind of feedback, which can lead to the sudden rocketing of heart-rate known as paroxysmal tachycardia. (The American writer Joyce Carol Oates suffers from this, and wrote about an attack in her essay 'Against Nature': 'When you discover yourself lying on the ground, limp and unresisting, head in the dirt, and helpless, the earth seems to shift forward as a presence; hard, emphatic, not mere surface but a genuine force . . . The outside wants to come in, and only the self's fragile membrane prevents it.')

The short-circuit was fortunately minimal in my case. The consultant was even able to pinpoint where it was on his diagram, and any anxiety I might have felt was cancelled out by the monogrammed particularity of this quirk, and the thought – obvious enough in retrospect – that one's inside wiring is as uniquely personal as one's external features. It was a new idea to me, the realisation that physical abnormality could be seen simply as difference, an aspect of biological diversity. When you add this to Groddeck's 'vital expression', it is a miracle human disorders are ever regular enough to be given names.

But symptoms are not purely personal. They are also a kind

of language, moulded by culture and fashion as well as bodily imperatives. In the Victorian era, for example, 'hysterical paralysis' was the psychosomatic symptom most often produced by women, and the favourite diagnosis by male doctors, doubtless reflecting the way the former's social roles were defined – and confined – by the latter. Today it has virtually vanished as a disorder, to be replaced by chronic fatigue.

Other modern symptom clusters have, understandably, an environmental accent. Asthma and allergies, for instance, are real and increasingly widespread responses to air and water pollution. But many purely psychosomatic complaints are now also viewed by sufferers as having environmental causes, despite being constructed out of hypochondria's traditional symptom pool.

The commonest complaint with a root in each camp is probably seasonal affective disorder. A slowing down of the whole metabolism is an almost universal human experience during winter, but between 5 and 10 per cent of the population suffer from marked lethargy, depression, irritability and weight gain. SAD is now believed to be brought on in susceptible individuals by the low levels of daylight in winter. Sunlight, acting via the pineal gland, shuts off the secretion of the hormone melatonin, and leaves levels of it and other brain chemicals, such as serotonin, close to the levels they are in sleep – or hibernation. In the late 1970s I spent a few nights at the BBC experimental Iron Age camp in Dorset. The volunteers lived in a large conical hut with a fire in the middle, and during long winter nights used to stay in bed for up to fifteen hours. There was not much work to be done at this time of year (they were living off their summer surpluses), but they were still an active and well-adjusted bunch when they did get up.

Perhaps this is the answer. Maybe SAD is not a disorder at all, but just an exaggeration of a normal reaction, and that what is at fault are our repeated attempts to override our physiology. The neurologist Oliver Sacks has suggested that some psychosomatic disorders might be civilised ornamentations of entirely natural states, especially of the biological response to stress that lies *between* fight and flight – the withdrawal that he calls 'vegetative retreat'. It is commoner in the natural world than we may think, in such states as feigning dead, freezing, defensive postures.

There is a growing approach to disease called 'evolutionary medicine', which is looking at how symptoms evolved, and whether they should always be viewed as 'ills' to be challenged or eradicated. Many are patently beneficial, however inconvenient: fever, for instance, which kills off invading bacteria. Others may be the result of compromises made during our evolution: back pain may be the price of an upright posture, and an inclination to panic attacks the price of having a nervous system alert to all kinds of danger.

Psychosomatic disorders may arise from the frequent mismatches between the contexts in which our physiology (nervous systems particularly) evolved and the contexts in which they have to operate now, especially all the vigilance and 'prepared responses' to danger encoded in the brain, which often no longer have a real focus outside ourselves. It is hard to see what other function they could fulfil. They are a nuisance to sufferers, and to their friends and doctors alike. They fuel a whole economy of spurious remedies and therapies. They don't even fade away, as psychoanalytic theory says they should, when you begin to understand what you use them for. Perhaps the over-strung aeolian harp is not such a bad model after all; there are some people who simply vibrate too much in emotional or circumstantial winds, and listen too attentively to the sound. If only we could be a bit more dispassionate about it, becoming real naturalists of the bodies we inhabit, hypochondria could become a source of fascination rather than morbid anxiety.

For myself, I am the opposite to Joyce Carol Oates, and feel closest to this acceptance just when the 'outside' begins to penetrate my own 'fragile membrane'. I find it hard to listen to a mistle thrush singing through a storm, or see the swifts returning in spring after a million miles on the wing, without experiencing, albeit vicariously, some of the suppleness and indomitability of nature in the face of all the fraying experiences of being alive.

1994

Acknowledgements

'Landscape: The Real Stuff' first appeared in *Towards a New Landscape*, Bernard Jacobson, 1993; 'Beeched' in the *Countryman* magazine; 'A Walk Around the Block' in *Walking in Britain*, ed. John Hillaby, William Collins, 1988; 'Beating the Bounds' in *The Times*; 'The Parish Map' and 'What Shapes a View?' in *Country Living*; 'Kew's Hurricane', 'The Roots of Civilisation', 'The Severn Estuary', 'A Limestone Landscape', 'Winter in the Camargue' and 'The Lubéron' in the *Sunday Times*; 'Devil's Meat' and 'the Wash' in the *Independent*.

'The Nature of Local Distinctiveness' is an edited version of a lecture delivered at Common Ground's conference on Local Distinctiveness in September 1993.

'A Chiltern Ramble' first appeared in *Rambling* magazine; 'A Perfect Weekend' in *Country Homes and Interiors*; 'Crete' and 'Don McCullin' in the *Sunday Telegraph*; 'Patrick Wright and the Heritage Question', 'Art and Ecology', 'William Tillyer', 'Christo' and 'Peter Fuller and Ruskin' in *Modern Painters*.

'Eric Ashby' is adapted from an introduction to *The Secret Life of the New Forest*, Eric Ashby, Chatto and Windus, 1989. 'Tony Evans' and all the material in 'A Sense of Occasion' are from *BBC Wildlife* magazine.

'James Lovelock and Gaia' was originally commissioned by

232

the *Sunday Times* but not published. 'SAD – A Natural History of Hypochondria' is a new piece based on an idea first published at much shorter length in the *Independent*.

My thanks to the editors who originally commissioned the above material.

My gratitute also to Pattie Barron, Vivien Green, Penny Hoare, Robin McIntosh and Richard Simon for their helpful comments on the text, and to Roger Cazalet for his meticulous editing.